MAIDEN WARRIOR MOTHER CRONE

Divine feminine archetypes for modern life

JULIE PETERS

Illustrated by
Nadia Murash

VERBENA

CONTENTS

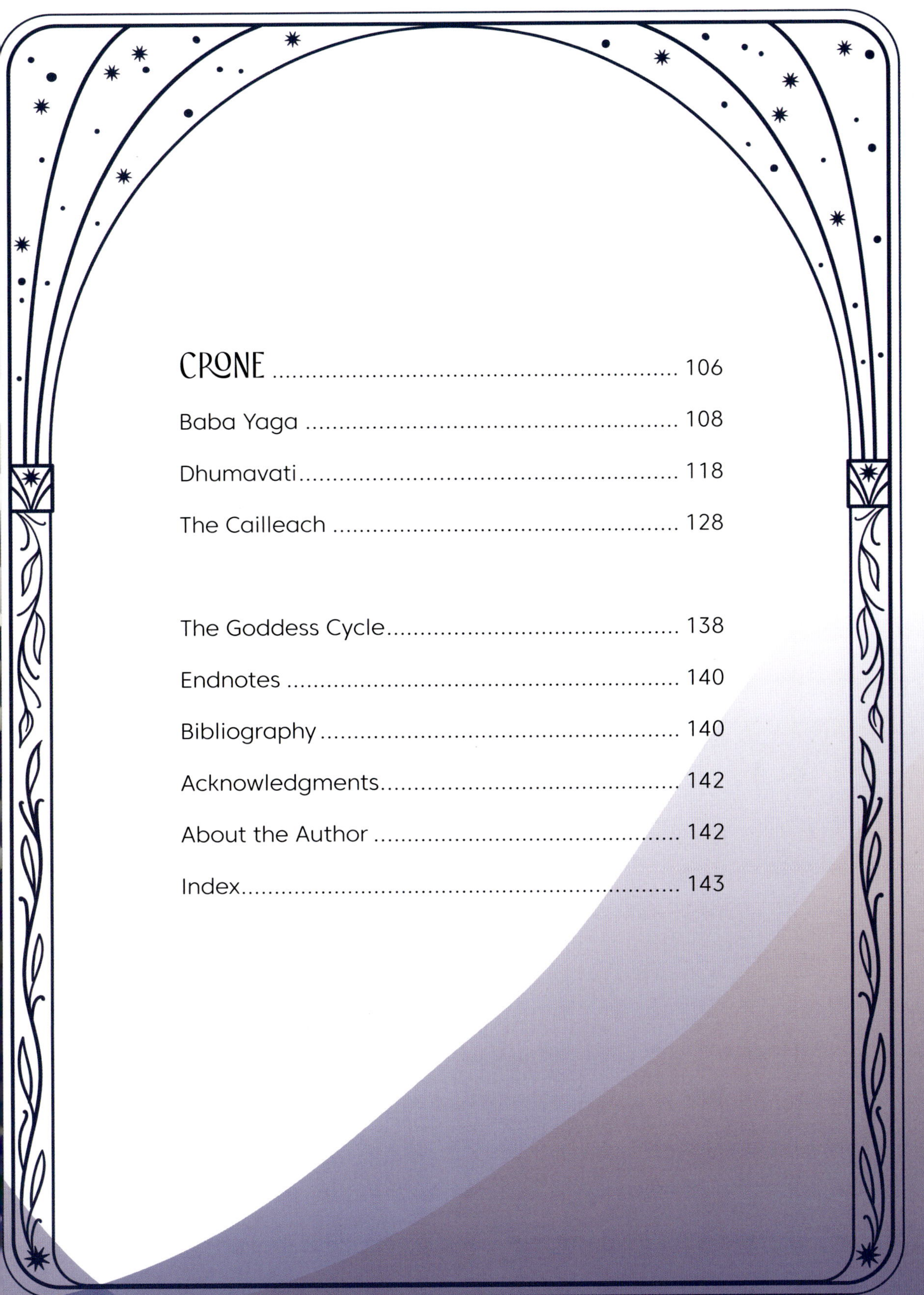

WELCOME

Once upon a time, God was a woman.

Since there have been people around to imagine, they have imagined a powerful feminine energy, a mysterious force that gave birth to the universe. The earliest evidence of human culture shows cave drawings and figurines that clearly honor the magic and miracle of the divine feminine and the unique power that is giving birth. These early cultures were likely matriarchal, and some of them were almost certainly peaceful, showing no evidence of weapons or war until another culture invaded, bringing in the concept of battle.

There's no way to know for sure what life was like in these cultures, but we do know that they imagined a Goddess. Sometimes she was sweet and beautiful, bringing in the joy of spring and summer as Maiden. Sometimes she was a fighter, ready to protect the land and the people as Warrior. Sometimes she was the creatrix of the Universe, giving birth to all as Mother. And sometimes she was Death and Endings, completing the cycle as Crone.

Today, in many parts of the world, a male god prevails. But we haven't forgotten about the divine feminine, no matter how often her name has changed. We may call her Inanna, Mary, the Cailleach, Universe, Cosmos, Great Mystery, Love, Energy, or any of the names you find in this book and beyond. A lot has changed since the early days when the Goddess was supreme. But the Goddess still lives.

MAIDEN, WARRIOR, MOTHER, CRONE

Many mythologies about goddesses involve a triplet: three sisters, three names, three versions of the divine feminine. Most commonly, this is Maiden, Mother, and Crone: the Goddess can be the potential and new birth of the springtime as Maiden, the life-giving abundance of Mother in the summer, and the representation of old age and endings as the Crone in the winter. These are powerful archetypes that play important roles in the cycles of the seasons, the Moon, and, to a degree, our lives.

Some people have extrapolated this triplicate to represent three phases of a woman's life. But these concepts frame her in relationship to others: the Maiden is married to a man who turns her into a Mother and then she shares her wisdom with the community as Crone. The Goddess has never been anything but one unto herself, able to create and destroy at her whim. She can hold these ideas for us, sure, slipping in and out of them as needed. But that's hardly all she is.

We're also missing one facet here: Warrior. In a pre-patriarchal society, before the first invasions invented the need to fight to protect our rights, our culture, and our selfhood, we may not have needed the Warrior archetype. But invasions and colonizations are cyclic, too, repeating over and over since they began. Graves have been found all over the world of women who were buried in battle armor with their weapons. Recent scientific evidence shows that women were as likely to be hunters as gatherers in early societies as men. Legends tell of powerful queens that led armies against invaders. Women have always fought for themselves, their children, and their people as long as there has been a need. But Warriors don't always wear armor.

When a culture is invaded, it's rarely eradicated. More often than not colonizers insert themselves into the pre-existing culture, intermarrying, teaching, learning, and re-shaping stories and customs until the two separate cultures become a single new one. One of the oldest strategies of war was to kill all the men in a given region and keep the women and children, building new families from the people who were left. Maidens needed to fight to protect their maidenhood. Mothers needed to fight for the survival of their children. And Crones needed to fight to hold onto the old ways. It was the women and children who had to find a way to be Warriors for who they were, whether that was through armor, song, ritual, art, or storytelling. It is thanks to those Warriors that we know the Goddess today, despite the many attempts to destroy, discredit, and suppress her.

This book isn't just about goddesses. It's also about queens, witches, heroines, and the many feminine figures that have shaped and expressed cultures all over the world for millennia. Regardless of your sex, gender, religion, land, or worldview, this book is also about you.

STORYTELLING

As the famous mythologist Joseph Campbell has written, "myths are public dreams, dreams are private myths." A myth tells an emotional or psychological truth without needing to be literally true. It can hold our fears, our hopes, and our imaginings about who we are and what it means to be alive (and, sometimes, to be dead). The stories about these divine feminine figures likely existed for a long time before they were ever written down, and their original authors are lost to the mists of time. Myths tend to shift and evolve depending on who is telling the story and what truth is needed in that moment. Details come and go, motifs are highlighted or slip into the shadows, and characters from different mythologies meet and interact as their cultures do. A myth is not a historically correct sequence of events. It's an artifact of time, place, and belief. It's a gift.

I grew up in Toronto, on Mississauga, Haudenosaunee, and Wendake land, the great-granddaughter of immigrants from England and Ireland. I would go to Sunday school and listen to boring stories about the Christian God, anxiously awaiting my chance to play Mary in the annual nativity play at Christmas—obviously, it seemed to me, the starring role in that show. Someone gave me a book of Greek mythology for children, and I read it to pieces. I still keep a place for its ragged pages on my bookshelf. I studied poetry and world religions at school, where I stared at Zen koans and visited churches with my feminist Christianity teacher, looking at art and talking with the class about how it made us feel. I devoted myself to yoga, where my teachers would tell stories of goddesses who were warriors with blue skin and bloody mouths, or beautiful, sexy mothers who would saunter up to a lion and destroy anyone who looked at them the wrong way. I became entranced with the Moon and collected

tarot decks, where strange images of divine feminine figures poked at a tender place in my heart. This is a place of deep longing, of the unspoken loss of the old ways, the ancient knowings that were overwritten by the Christians so long ago no one in my family can remember them. But my bones remember them. My dreams remember them. Some part of me knew, even as a child, that there was more to Mary than her starring role in the nativity play.

As I've gotten to know and love these divine feminine figures from across the world, I've held their stories in my heart and written them into this book from my imagination. Don't think of these tales as authoritative. Think of them as imaginative. Receive these stories against your own deep truths, your private myths, and our shared public dreams.

MEDITATIONS

At the end of each chapter in this book, there is a meditation you can do to hold the story in your own heart and imagination, in your own way. If you'd like to do this, prepare a simple space for your meditation. You can sit or lie down and do it in any space that works for you. If you have an altar, feel free to do it there. I may have suggestions for items to include in your meditation process, but if you want to add in any specific items or practices from your traditional or inner knowings, feel free to add these. Lighting a candle helps to create an intentional space.

Acknowledge the land that you are on and your relationship with this land. Consider where your family and people came from, as far back as you're aware, and how you made it here. Notice the quality of the light today, the season, the weather, and the phase of the Moon. Remember yourself as an integral part of the web of everything.

You may also want to consider the land of the goddess or divine feminine figure you're working with. Think about where that is or was in the world, if you've ever been there, if you have ancestors from there that you know about, and if the land has other names that you know of. Notice how thinking about that land, that climate, or that part of the world resonates with you as you think about it now.

Then imagine a circle of protection around you. You can do this literally if you like, with salt, stones, or chalk, but it's not necessary. Set the clear intention that only energies that are in alignment with your highest good and the highest good of all may enter this circle; anything that is not in that alignment stays outside of the circle.

When your meditation is complete, thank the land, the circle, the goddess or divine feminine figure you've been working with, and anyone or anything else you'd like to offer gratitude towards. You can finish with words that feel right to you. Here are a few examples:

IT'S TIME TO MEET THE MAIDEN, THE WARRIOR, THE MOTHER, AND THE CRONE. LET'S IMAGINE HER TOGETHER.

MAIDEN

The Maiden archetype represents potential. She holds the qualities of energy, possibility, the new green shoot just beginning to poke up out of the dirt. She is innocence that almost always comes to learn through experience. She is traditionally represented in the waxing moon, but I would also place her at the new moon, where she is in the darkness, just about to reach out to the light.

PERSEPHONE'S CALL TO THE UNDERWORLD

Persephone was as beautiful as her mother, with long, loose hair like corn silk, skin as smooth as fresh milk, and eyes the blue of cornflowers. She was known as Kore, the Maiden, and the goddess Demeter's beloved only daughter.

Persephone would spend her days playing in the woods with the wild animals, flowers, nymphs, and dryads of Demeter's realm. Some days, she would get quiet and listen to them talk to each other, which is how she heard the tales of her mother, the goddess of grain, and why they never went to Mount Olympus where the rest of her mother's family lived. She heard that the great god Zeus, her mother's brother, had done something terrible to Demeter. After that, she'd made her home on the ground where she could tend to the fruits and flowers of the Earth, planting the seeds, and pruning the trees.

Persephone loved her life as it was, but she often wondered. She wondered about Olympus and the gods up there. She also wondered about what was beneath her, what happened to the seeds when they went into the dark earth and then mysteriously broke ground some time later.

When Demeter gave her a handful of seeds, Persephone would gently part the earth and plant them inside. She would cover them up with the soft dirt and whisper to them, telling them that everything would be alright, that they would know just what to do in the dark.

Then she would lay on her belly and press her ear to the ground, seeing if she could hear the seeds whisper back. Sometimes she did hear something. It wasn't like whispering, not like anything she'd ever heard before. A song she couldn't quite place. A call, a tune, a prayer? She didn't know, but she would stay like that for a long time, eyes closed, listening.

One night, Persephone was laying on the earth, as was her custom, listening to the strange underground song, when it suddenly spoke: "Do you want to know?" It startled the girl so much that she bolted upright and ran, not knowing whether she was running away or towards something. Finally, she slowed, and found herself in a beautiful glen that she'd never seen before. It was dark and quiet, strangely beautiful, and in the center were growing the most beautiful flowers she had ever seen in her life. They were deep purple and blood red, perfect and strange, like a shadowy version of the bright yellowy narcissus she knew so well.

As she leaned down to cup her hands around the strange flowers, the earth opened into a great chasm, and the darkly handsome god Hades appeared before her. He was driving a golden chariot pulled by four steeds as black as night. Without a word, he gathered her up and took her with him, the earth swallowing them both.

With Persephone gone, the glen again went quiet. The narcissus flowers wilted, leaning their sorry cheeks against the earth as if in mourning. The bright moon darkened and a new chill shivered through the air.

Demeter could not understand what had happened to her beautiful daughter. She called and called for her, desperately seeking for her beloved child. She wept, her salt tears stinging the dirt. She stopped tending to the fruit and flowers of the Earth, withdrawing her fertile energy, and the ground became cold and quiet. No corn grew in the fields. No animals approached each other, stopping the flow of milk or young. The land appeared to die all around Demeter, as if it was mourning with her.

Months passed, and the gods began to miss their sacrifices. Demeter's friend Hekate, goddess of magic, was worried. They had been searching together for ten days and ten nights, and they were exhausted. Hekate spoke:

"Dear friend. There is one place we haven't looked."

Demeter looked up at her friend, expectant.

"I was afraid to say anything because I wasn't sure. But the night Persephone went missing, I heard a great crack in the Earth. I suspect Persephone is in the Underworld with Hades, who wanted her hand in marriage so much."

Demeter's eyes went black with fury, immediately knowing her friend was right. She had known Hades had his eye on her daughter, as had everyone else, and her efforts to protect her from the violence she had endured at the hands of men had, at last, failed.

Demeter knew she could not follow her daughter to the Underworld, but she could have words with her brother, Zeus. She flew up to Olympus, rage in her heart for what had been done to her and her daughter, and to so many others. Zeus knew the moment he saw her the reason his sister had come to his throne.

"Return her to me," Demeter said, her jaw tight, "or I shall never attend the Earth again. You shall never receive another sacrifice from one of your beloved starving humans."

Zeus knew better than to further push the goddess of the land and human life. Zeus called for Hermes, the messenger, to go down to the Underworld and retrieve his sister's daughter.

When Hermes arrived in the Underworld, he found Hades and Persephone walking the halls together, deep in conversation, close, but not touching. He noticed that she kept her eyes averted from his gaze until he looked away, and then she would stare at his face, a slight blush coming over her cheeks. Hermes watched as she spoke to a newly dead soul, soothing them, helping them to enter their new existence without fear. She looked uncannily like a queen of the Underworld.

Hermes sat the two down, explaining that Zeus wanted Persephone to return to the world above, to be with her mother. As Persephone learned that she could go home now, she was surprised to find she wasn't sure she wanted to. She loved the Underworld. It was where the song that had been haunting her for so long had been coming from. She had found that she had a special talent for welcoming the dead into their new home, helping to soothe and nurture these very different underground seeds than the ones she used to whisper to in the above world. Despite the suddenness of his abduction, Hades had been kind to her, seeming to regret causing her fear but unsure of how to make her feel comfortable. Persephone looked at Hades, unsure of what to do.

The god of the Underworld seemed to understand her right away without needing to hear her speak. He picked up a bowl of fresh pomegranate seeds and offered it to her. "My dear, you are free to leave if you wish. But before you go, eat some of my food. It will keep you connected to me and to this world forever."

Persephone plucked six pomegranate seeds from the bowl and put them in her mouth, savoring the sweet and sour taste of the seeds. It was the first food she had eaten in the Underworld, knowing this choice would bring her back to Hades and his mysterious dark realm. Then she took Hermes' hand and allowed him to take her home to her mother.

When at last Demeter could hold her daughter again, Persephone wept as her mother wept. These tears of joy refilled the rivers and ponds with fresh, new water, nourishing the earth, beginning the process of bringing the land back to life. The new shoots again began to push through the dirt, the grapes began to ripen on the vine, the animals began to turn to each other once again, creating milk and young, and the gods would once again receive the smoke from the humans' sacrifices.

But an agreement had to be made. For the six pomegranate seeds that Persephone ate, she would spend six months of each year in the below world with Hades, who would indeed become her husband. There, she would welcome the dead, helping them to transition into this new realm. Though her mother continued to grieve each year, filled with winter-making rage and sorrow, each year she would return to joy with her daughter, bringing life back to Earth as spring and summer. When she slept in one place, Persephone would dream of the other, knowing she was a goddess of above and below, of death and life, not merely the Kore Maiden anymore. As a Maiden, Persephone had wanted to know the song of the dead. Now she was their Queen.

CHTHONIC DEMETER

You may know some pieces of Persephone's story, a tale often called "The Rape of Persephone" as found in the *Homeric Hymns* compiled in the seventh century BCE. This story tells of the sudden abduction of Persephone by the desirous god Hades, causing her mother Demeter such grief that she essentially invents winter. Persephone is a hapless victim and winter is a punishment for everyone.

But there may be an older understanding of Persephone's myth that doesn't quite align with this sad tale. There is evidence that Demeter's cult is ancient, older than that of Zeus and the other male gods, and has obvious links to the older goddesses Gaia and Isis (who are, in turn, related to Ishtar and Inanna). While Demeter is the goddess of grain and agriculture, she is also a goddess of the Underworld, where her plants must begin before they can hit the surface and grow. In some areas of Greece, this goddess was known as *Demeter Chthonia*, which means something like "Demeter of the Underworld", and in Athens, the dead were called *Demetreoi*, a word that means "Demeter's people." In Charlene Spretnak's telling of the tale in her book *Lost Goddesses of Early Greece*, there is no Zeus or Hades. Persephone tells her mother of her desire to go to the Underworld and tend to the newly dead souls she's heard moaning for help from beneath the fertile earth. Demeter responds,

> "It is I who have domain over the Underworld. From beneath the surface of the earth I draw forth the crops and the wild plants. And in pits beneath the surface of the earth I have instructed the mortals to store my seed from harvest until sowing, in order that contact with the spirits of my Underworld will fertilize the seed. Yes, I know very well the realm of the dead, but my most important work is here. I must feed the living."

Demeter may have been, like many pre-patriarchal goddesses, sovereign over both life and death. The "Rape of Persephone" may refer to a different kind of invasion, which is that of the patriarchal Zeus-worshippers over the indigenous goddess religions of early Greece. This cultural shift may have forced this ancient goddess into two: the Mother, Demeter, and the "Kore", the Maiden, Persephone, who must take on the death role that Demeter could no longer hold on her own.

This story could have been told without any of the male gods involved. But my interpretation here—which is heavily influenced by that of teacher and mythologist Natalie Rousseau—invites the possibility of romance. This romance is not only the draw between Hades and Persephone, but between Persephone and the truth, her calling, her desire to know. Perhaps the song of the Underworld brought her to exactly where she was meant to be, bringing the cyclic wisdom of the seasons into a world that suffers in its sameness.

PERSEPHONE AND THE SONG OF THE UNDERWORLD

When we listen to a call deep in our hearts to change something, to move from the stable status quo to something strange and unknown, we may certainly be terrified. Life is hard enough, and many of us choose the easy route to keep things as safe and stable as possible. But when that call is strong enough, we often find that we must know what's speaking to us beneath the flowers. We must find out what happens if we break a rule or go a different way or fight back against something that others have simply accepted. It's a new, strange path that will not allow you to turn back, but only forward, only through. We may indeed need to meet the underside of the world we've always taken for granted. But we may also discover that there is food there—the delicious, ripe pomegranate seeds that seal Persephone's fate. Go ahead and eat the food of the other world: you will learn things that may change you, but you will never want to go back to the way things were before.

MEDITATION WITH PERSEPHONE:

Answering the call

Get settled for your meditation. Acknowledge the land, the land of your people, and the lands of Demeter and Persephone. Set your circle. Light a candle if you wish.

Take a few deep breaths and begin to turn your attention to your heart. Listen inwardly.

When you're ready, turn your attention to the concept of your calling. We don't need to think of this as one specific thing you're meant to do in your life, but think about what's calling you now. What do you love? What would you be doing if you had all the time in the world, no obligations, if money was not a factor?

For now, let's drop into another world, where none of those rules apply. Simply listen for the song that's calling you towards it. What is most important in your life right now? What are your natural talents? What comes easily to you? What gives you joy?

What would it look like to devote yourself more fully to this aspect of who you are? What would have to change within you or outside of you in order to offer yourself to this place? What might have to die so that this part of you can live?

Take your time with these questions. When you feel complete with the meditation, take a few deep breaths, thanking the land, the earth, the sky, your circle of protection, and your own heart for talking to you. When you're ready, open your eyes. If you wish, journal about what you learned.

INANNA'S DESCENT INTO THE UNDERWORLD

Inanna is the Queen of Heaven. The Daughter of the Moon. She is the Empress of Desire, the one who calls forward the look of wanting that comes over the cows and sheep, the bees who want to touch the beauty of the flowers, spreading their pollen from bloom to bloom, the deep yearning of the underground seed to push towards the warmth of the Sun at the surface. She is the one who draws out the warlike greed for power that overcomes those who want the lands of another. She incites the irresistible desire to know, even (and especially) when it might cause a little trouble.

As the Queen of Heaven, Inanna had everything. She was powerful over the earth and sky. And yet there was one realm she did not know—the Underworld, the deep below that her sister, Ereshkigal, had claimed. Every now and then, when she was alone, Inanna would lay belly down and put her ear to the ground, listening for the curious sounds of the dead. Did they howl or cry? Were they silent? Inanna knew nothing if not desire. And she desired to know.

So it was that one day she decided to journey to the gates of Ereshkigal's Underworld. She told her friend Ninshubur, the Queen of the East, to look for her if she did not return in three days' time. Ninshubur worried, but knew better than to argue with her friend.

Inanna dressed herself in her most queenly finery, preparing for her adventure. She chanted the magic words:

> "From the Great Above she opened her ear to the Great Below. From the Great Above the goddess opened her ear to the Great Below. From the Great Above Inanna opened her ear to the Great Below."[1]

Inanna stood in the moonlight, waiting. Neti, the gatekeeper of Ereshkigal's realm, appeared.

"Who are you? And why do you come to the Land of No Return?"

"I am Inanna, Queen of Heaven," she stated. "I come to visit my sister."

Neti nodded and opened the first gate, requesting the great horned crown that connected Inanna to the Anunnuki, all the gods and goddesses of her lineage as Daughter of the Moon.

Inanna handed Neti her crown.

At the second gate, he requested her headdress, the delicate weave of lapis that threaded down through her dark hair like a weave of stars, marking her ability to see clearly, to know herself as the Queen of Heaven.

Inanna handed Neti her headdress.

At the third gate, he requested her necklace, the rainbow that adorned her throat, the marker of her power as a goddess to speak what she wishes and make it come true.

Inanna handed Neti her necklace.

At the fourth gate, he requested her breastplate, adorned with the darkest jewels of lapis, connecting her to the ocean and the sky, her powers over love in the above world.

Inanna handed Neti her breastplate.

At the fifth gate, he requested her girdle, adorned with the signs of the zodiac, marking her power over the movements of time through the solar year.

Inanna handed Neti her girdle.

At the sixth gate, he requested her dress, including the loincloth keeping her sacred womb protected, her ability to call forth the fertility of the people, land, and animals of the above world.

Inanna handed Neti her dress.

At the seventh gate, he requested her sandals, her last humble connection to the earth and the world she reigned over as a queen.

Inanna handed Neti her sandals.

At last, Inanna entered the Underworld, bowed low, completely nude, stripped of all the markers of her power and identity as Queen. Inanna faced her sister like the dead who eat clay for their dinner and drink dust as their wine. Ereshkigal looked at her sister, her eyes piercing and powerful, her question silent but clear.

Inanna did not return her gaze, at first, knowing that she had gone deeper into her quest than she'd ever really expected to. She could now see that while she ruled love and war, her sister ruled life and death. She dropped to her knees, bowing deeply.

"Even now, my sister, you do not understand," Ereshkigal said softly. "Do you truly want to know?"

Inanna turned her face to her sister and met her gaze at last. Despite her fear, Inanna's desire to know was absolute.

"Yes." She spoke clearly and simply.

"Very well then." Ereshkigal fastened the eye of death upon Inanna and her attendants hung her corpse from a hook on the wall like so much rotting meat.

At this moment in the world above, a pall took over the land. Leaves stiffened, dried, and fell from the trees. Flowers wilted, turning underground as if to rest. The bull did not turn to the cow. Men and women did not look at each other with desire. The Moon turned its face away in darkness. Everything living fell into a wintry sleep.

Ninshubur knew that her friend was in trouble. She appealed to the temple of Enlil, god of wind and air, to help her, and he merely laughed, shaking his head at Inanna's foolishness. She went to the temple of Nanna, the Moon, Inanna's own father, and while his face darkened, he shook his head as if he'd known this would one day happen. She tried the temple of Anu, god of the sky, who barely seemed to hear her pleas.

Finally, Ninshubur appealed to Enki, god of sky, water, and earth. Enki saw that, without Inanna, his earth and water could not come together to create life. He agreed to help, and created two beings from the dirt under his fingernails to go and retrieve the goddess.

"Offer Ereshkigal whatever she wants in exchange for Inanna's corpse, then sprinkle the water and food of life over her body so she returns to us," he instructed them.

The two creatures, which were neither male nor female, flew into the Underworld, slipping through cracks in the gates like flies. They found Ereshkigal there in the agony of giving birth.

"Oh, my insides!" She cried.

"Oh, your insides!" The creatures cried.

"Oh, my outsides!" She cried.

"Oh, my outsides!" They responded.[2]

"Who are you that moans and cries with me? I have been alone and mourning the death of my husband, and you sympathize with me. I shall offer you a gift."

“We wish only for the corpse on the wall,” the creatures replied.

“She gave herself to me,” Ereshkigal growled as her labor pains struck up again. “She wanted to know.”

Still, the creatures insisted, and the exhausted Ereshkigal agreed to let Inanna down from the hook.

As the Queen of the Underworld settled, her pain easing, the creatures sprinkled Inanna’s body with the water of life. Breath returned to Inanna’s body. They brought her back through the gates of the Underworld, and as each piece of her dress and jewelry was returned to her, she revived a little bit more. When at last her crown was placed on her head, desire sparked once again in her body. The Queen of Heaven and Earth had returned.

But as a debt of life has been given, a debt of death must be paid. Shadowy Underworld creatures called *galla* followed Inanna back to her palace, seeking someone to take her place. As soon as Inanna embraced her friend and rescuer, Ninshubur, the *galla* tugged at her dress. Back to full strength and fury, however, Inanna quickly struck them away from her friend. So the creatures turned to Inanna’s attendants, who were dressed in mourning clothes and weeping for joy that their beloved queen had returned. Again, Inanna struck them away, protecting the attendants who had mourned her properly. But when Inanna arrived at her throne, she found her husband Dumuzi sitting in her place, dressed in finery, accepting sweet grapes from the gentle hands of his servant girls, not mourning his queen as he should. Inanna fastened the eye of death upon him, and the *galla* knew they had found their life debt at last.

As she watched her husband get taken away to the Underworld, crying out in fear and pain, Inanna regretted her rash decision. She knew now what the Underworld was like and how close she was to being there forever. Inanna wept, and Ninshubur wept with her. Dumuzi’s sister, Geshtinanna, and his mother, Sirtur, joined them in their lamentations. With Inanna wrapped up in her grief, the Moon stayed dark and the world stayed cold and lifeless.

Days passed, and the women wept. Inanna wept for her husband, but also for her mistakes, her rashness, for all she didn't understand before all this came to pass. At last a tiny fly came into the mourning room and buzzed in Inanna's ear. It told her where Dumuzi was and to go there. The three women followed the fly to find Dumuzi at the gates of the Underworld, naked and pale. From the shadows appeared the venerable Ereshkigal, beautiful and dark.

"I know you must reign over your world, sister, as I must reign over mine. I know the pain of loss as you now know it. If you do not wish to leave Dumuzi here in your place, you must choose someone else. My rules are as unmoving as yours."

Inanna bowed to her sister's power and sovereignty. But she remained silent, not knowing what to do.

"I will go," offered Geshtinanna. "I will go."

"For half the year," Inanna conceded. "For half the year you will go in Dumuzi's place. The other half, you will return to life and Dumuzi will die again. I will mourn every year in honor of my husband, his sister, and my sister, Queen Ereshkigal."

So it was that the world came back to life, with bees pollinating the flowers, bulls impregnating the cows, and men and women dancing and celebrating with each other with desire and joy in the sunlight. But then the world would cycle into cold and darkness, a quiet winter, holding a little of the wisdom of Ereshkigal's Underworld. Inanna had brought a touch of death and loss into her world of life and love. But she had wanted to know, and now she held that knowledge more precious than any of the jewels and finery that had been returned to her body as queen.

THE LESSONS OF THE UNDERWORLD

Inanna is one of the oldest goddesses in the world, dating back to at least 4000 BCE. She evolved into the later goddess Ishtar and likely influenced Aphrodite, the Greek goddess of beauty, love, and sexuality. We also see echoes of her in Persephone, whose descent into the Underworld created seasonal winter.

It's unclear why, exactly, Inanna decides to go down to the Underworld. In some versions of her story she wants to honor the funeral rites of Ereshkigal's husband (whose death she caused in an earlier adventure). In others it's implied that she is power hungry, wanting to take over Ereshkigal's world. But as the goddess of desire, it makes sense to me that she couldn't bear that there was a whole realm she didn't know anything about.

It's significant that Ereshikigal, the goddess of death, is giving birth when Inanna is rescued. It's a reminder that birth and death are intimately connected. Inanna's experience ends eternal spring, but it also brings in the wisdom of fall and winter, the joy of the height of summer, the deep quiet of the new moon, and the learning we must do as human beings that are born and must, inevitably, die. Like Persephone and Demeter, Ereshkigal and Inanna could be understood as two sides of the same coin, two versions of the same goddess. Like the natural world we experience every day, life can be abundant, sweet, and benevolent, but it can also be cruel, cold, and biting. Many goddesses of love and life also rule war and death—this is true of the ancient goddesses Astarte and Ishtar as well as the Celtic goddess the Morrígan, who has a relationship with both fertility and battle.

Ereshkigal could be read as a villain here, but I see her as a kindred spirit, a wise one who gifts Inanna the knowledge she wanted, in part by gifting her with the consequences of her actions. As a goddess of birth, Inanna is incomplete without an understanding of death.

CYCLES OF GRIEF

Inanna's story is about loss, grief, and trauma, among other things. We all spend time in the Underworld at some point, and may even feel we are suspended there as if hung by a hook like so much meat. The feeling that grief could turn the whole world to ice and stone is deeply relatable. It can feel like the sun shines on everyone but us, our food tasting like clay, drinking the wine of dust. We feel that we are walking that moonlit path alone, that no one can join us there, no one can understand what we're really going through. Inanna had to walk this path alone, stripped of everything she thought made her who she was.

Inanna learns a lot from her dark journey, and she re-emerges as a wiser queen, one who better understands the world she rules because of the world she doesn't. No one would choose to go through the dark paths of grief, death, and trauma, but when we come out on the other side, we are often more compassionate, wiser, more able to tell when someone else is walking that moonlit path. The world may no longer be purely flowers and sunshine, but there's beauty in the rain.

MEDITATION WITH INANNA:

Descent into the Underworld

This meditation is best in a dark place, at night, on a new moon or the winter solstice, with an unlit candle and a lighter nearby. Difficult emotions can come up in the dark, so ensure you feel resourced enough to invite that. Honor and acknowledge the land and set your circle. Take a few deep breaths and settle in.

Receive the experience of being in the dark. Maybe you see yourself in the desert, in the dark of a wood, deep in an underground cave, even in Ereshkigal's Underworld. Sink into this dark place. Call to mind whatever has brought you into your own Underworld—grief, loss, difficulty, or emotional pain. Imagine Ereshkigal here with you. Keep breathing.

What lessons have you learned from this Underworld experience? What assumptions, expectations, or worldviews are being challenged? What strengths or abilities have you found within yourself?

Now invite Inanna. She is beautiful and strong, but wise from having been where you have been. She is a lighter, brighter version of the Underworld goddess, but all the more beautiful for having met her dark twin. See Inanna offering her hand to you, leading you up the steps into the above world again. She is not rejecting the Underworld lessons. She is bringing them up into the light.

Open your eyes and light your candle. Notice how it feels to bring this soft light back into this dark place. Think about what you're grateful for, what resources you have in your life, and what you're hoping for in the future. Stay here as long as you need to. Journal if you like. Thank Inanna and Ereshkigal for being with you in the darkness and the light.

EVE'S EXILE

Eve was born perfect. Flawless. Created from Adam's rib, she was meant to be a companion, a helpmeet, an obedient wife. A perfect woman born into a perfect place: Eden, a garden of abundance and plenty. All the animals here were friendly, all the plants eatable. Everything was delicious and perfect. And the same. Day after day, Adam pruned the perfect trees, and Eve would catch the branches. Night after night, they would eat the fruits of the garden, make perfect love, and sleep on the soft perfect ground. Morning after morning, they would greet the sun and God and feel that all was right with the world. Over and over. And over again.

And Adam was perfect. He'd tell Eve he loved her, that she was the only, the ideal, the one wife for him forever. But sometimes it felt to Eve as if something was hidden in his mouth, some reason he needed to reassure her she was the only one. Eve was told she was the first, and yet she couldn't help but feel there had been something before her here, in Eden, some seeds left by a rival somewhere, a shadow rustling behind a tree, a forbidden feeling that made her wonder if she was, indeed, the first. If she was even perfect at all.

And then there was the serpent. A beautiful asp, eyes like gemstones, scales reflecting every color. The snake felt different somehow, older than everything else in Eden, and Eve loved her. Eve and Serpent would talk for hours on their bellies in the shade of the flowers when Adam was busy tending to the garden. Serpent told her stories about wonders like loss, strife, and evil, and Eve was captivated.

One day, Eve told Serpent about her feeling that she was not, indeed, the first, that there had been something here before her, and Serpent told her stories. Wondrous stories of earth goddesses who appeared from nothing, ages where there were no gods or Adams, just, earth, sky, and stars. Queens who had royal subjects. Women who ruled the land of the dead. Eve asked Serpent if she was, in fact, one of these powerful beings, and she merely blinked her beautiful gemstone eyes, refusing to answer. On this day, though, Serpent had another idea. She turned her beautiful head and licked her tongue towards the Tree of Knowledge. This was the one rule of the garden of Eden, that Adam and Eve must not eat the fruit of the Tree of Knowledge, or they should die. Eve laughed her perfect, pealing laugh and reminded her friend of this rule.

"And why, my dear Eve, do you think that is the one rule here?"

Eve paused, sitting with the delightfully uncomfortable feeling that the asp often brought to her. She would say things that would cause Eve's mind to stretch with a strange painful pleasure. It was the only change, the only newness that the garden offered, and she loved Serpent for that. Eve voiced her thoughts. "Well, the fruit of the Tree of Knowledge would give us knowledge. It would allow us to know more, to understand more, to become capable of thinking in new ways."

"And would you like that, Eve?" Serpent asked.

"Oh, desperately, my friend. Desperately." She looked over at the Tree of Knowledge, its fruit clustered dark yellow and heavy, nearly bursting with sap that looked sweet and cool and smooth.

"And is this not your perfect place? A place where you can have anything you want?" Serpent blinked at Eve.

"I'm not so sure anymore," Eve told her friend. "I have this feeling inside sometimes, like when a rabbit gets caught in the bushes for a time before we untangle her. I am struggling, writhing, wanting to stretch out of my skin. I know this place is perfect. I love it. I love

Adam. I love God. I love all the animals and plants here, including you, my Serpent, my friend. I am grateful for everything I have. And yet..." Eve's eyes went soft, looking off towards the forbidden tree.

Serpent merely waited, listening.

"It is the same every day. It begins to feel like a lovely trap, like a place you cannot move at all. I can't help but feel..."

"That there's more?"

Eve turned towards her friend again. "Do you know that feeling, Serpent?"

"I do, my friend. I do." The serpent looked sad all of a sudden, and placed her jeweled head lightly on Eve's lap. They sat together in this indescribable sadness for a time.

"Perhaps we should eat of it," Eve said all of a sudden. "I feel I must know about good and evil. I must know what happens if I break a rule. I want to understand."

"God is not always kind, in my experience," Serpent said gently. "Rules broken cannot be unbroken."

"You're right," said Eve, her shoulders falling. "I shouldn't break the rule. I should stay here in paradise forever, never changing, never trying anything new. Adam's perfect wife. God's perfect daughter. Nothing but perfection around me. Why would I want to change it?" Fat, pearlescent tears ran down Eve's cheeks, landing on Serpent's head. Serpent couldn't bear to see her friend so sad, and she knew just what she was feeling. Serpent knew that Eve didn't have to stay here forever, but she knew she couldn't make the choice for her.

While Eve cried, Serpent slid over to the Tree of Knowledge and wound up its trunk, shaking loose one of its ripe, juicy fruits. She collected it in her body and brought it to the crying Eve. "You do have a choice, my friend. Do you want to know?" she asked, her eyes wide with compassion and empathy.

Eve became determined, all of a sudden, her brow furrowed, her jaw set. She picked up the fruit, pressed her nose to it. It had a delicate, sweet, complex scent, different from all the other fruits in Eden. She took a bite, allowing the juice to run down her chin, tasting its tang, swallowing its sweet flesh. Serpent watched as ecstasy and pain crossed Eve's face. There was loss and sorrow, joy and pride, and Eve's most precious desire, learning. She shuddered in pleasure and confusion. "What is this?" She finally asked.

"It is knowledge," said Serpent, fearful that she'd hurt her friend, hoping she'd done the right thing. "It is choice. It is knowing that you do not have to follow all the rules someone else set out for you. It is power. It is what connects you and me to the world that was here before God and his rules. Do you see it now?"

Eve nodded, her eyes filling with a different kind of tears, recognizing the Serpent now as Sister. Questioning everything. She gasped. "I must share this with Adam. He needs to know."

Eve ran to Adam who was tending to the trees and bushes of Eden, a slight sweat on his brow, a blissful smile on his face. When he turned to Eve he could see that she was different and his face clouded. "My love, what's wrong?"

"It's not that something is wrong," she panted. "It's that something is right. I have tasted the fruit of the Tree of Knowledge. I can feel the world outside of Eden. It is beautiful and horrible. It is old and new and not yet created. It is everything I've wanted to know. You must come with me. You must taste."

"I must not!" Adam cried. "God gave us a rule. He told us we'd die if we tasted this fruit. This could destroy our Eden, our love, our life!"

Eve was silent, feeling herself withdraw internally, a strange new feeling. Adam didn't understand her. She felt separate from him. Unwanted. Unloved. He didn't want to come with her to this new land of choice. Adam saw her harden slightly, recoiling from him. He'd never felt anything from her but love and desire. It made him panic.

"Wait, my love. Don't leave me. Help me understand. I love you. I would do anything for you."

"I want you to understand," she said. "But I want you to want to understand. I can see now that this fruit is taking me away from you. I cannot live in this relentless perfection anymore. I need more. And I want you to come with me. But I understand if you cannot."

Adam walked up to her, nothing but love and hope in his eyes. He held Eve's hand, heavy with the sticky sweet fruit, and drew it up to his face. "I love you more than anything. More than Eden. More than rules. I will go anywhere with you, Mother of All Living." Eve shuddered as she heard that name, not knowing what it meant, but knowing it was hers. Adam did know something more than what was here in Eden, after all.

Adam lifted her hand to his mouth and bit into the fruit. Runnels of juice ran down his chin and into her palm as the shadows of understanding, fear, shame, happiness, and other complex emotions crossed the depths of his eyes. She kissed him deeply, tasting the sweetness of the fruit on his lips, loving him more than ever, grateful that he would try to understand with her, that he wanted to go with her into this forbidden place.

Serpent watched as God appeared, tears in his eyes, rage on his brow. She knew he would not like that his new creations desired to be separate from him, to learn their own lessons and live their own lives. But she could see that he expected it somehow—otherwise why would he put the Tree of Knowledge right in the center of the garden, its fruits so heavy and ripe with temptation? Serpent worried for her friend as God handed Adam and Eve their consequences, which included death and life. Eve could now know the joy and pain of motherhood. She would now have to learn about the land outside of Eden and what it takes to pull food from hard soil. Serpent watched Eve, squeezing Adam's hand, terrified and ready, knowing these punishments were actually difficult gifts. At last, God opened the gates of Eden. He called it exile. Eve knew it was freedom.

ALL ABOUT EVE

Eve is the first woman, in Hebrew and Christian mythology. Her story is told in the Bible's Old Testament, a text held sacred by Judaism, Christianity, and several other faiths that could date back to the Iron Age (1200 BCE) or earlier. The book of Genesis, where Eve appears in writing, was likely completed around the fifth century BCE. Eve's image, often with an apple in her hand and a serpent twining a tree nearby, is ubiquitous. She is revered as our ancient Mother of All Living, as Adam names her, but also derided as the one who ruined our perfect relationship with God. For some, Eve invented the concept of free will: perhaps we'd be happier in some paradise where every day is the same and everything is done for us. But we're human beings, living on a difficult Earth. Curiosity, learning, and growth is, maybe, what separates humans from other animals—we keep trying, keep failing, and keep growing and changing as we try again.

The standard interpretation of this myth is that Eve is to blame for humanity's fall from paradise. Adam is punished with having to till the hard land for his food, and Eve gets this particularly chilling curse: "I will greatly multiply your pain in childbearing; in pain you shall bring forth children, yet your desire shall be for your husband, and he shall rule over you" (Genesis 3:16). As Merlin Stone writes in her book *When God Was a Woman*, "Thus my penitent, submissive position as a female was firmly established by page three of the nearly one thousand pages of the Judeo-Christian Bible."

It's important to understand that the Bible is a man-made product. It is a collection of stories, parables, and poetry from many sources over a significant range of time. It has been translated into many languages, and, inevitably, some things are lost in translation. The writers and translators of the Bible were flawed human beings with biases, assumptions, and, in some cases, clear religious and political agendas. Some of them were likely writing down stories that had been told orally for generations—the same mechanism through which we get most myths. Some of these stories included symbols and motifs from older mythologies. Some say these stories came to the writers in prayer or meditation, making them seem like the word of God. So we must take this work with a grain (or pillar?) of salt.

There is plenty of evidence that some biblical writings attempt to discredit the goddess-oriented belief structures that were more present and powerful at the time. The first of the Ten Commandments is "Thou shalt have no other gods before me," which implies that there were other gods around. The false idols that are so commonly warned against in the Bible were likely the ubiquitous images of female goddesses that predate the Bible by thousands of years. You've probably seen the paleolithic Venus figurines that were found all over the world from about 26,000 years ago. These could have been some of those idols. In fact, it's likely that the serpent in the garden of Eden represents the ancient goddess. Serpents were important symbols for Inanna, Ishtar, Isis, and many other goddesses. They represented fertility, wisdom, healing, and rebirth. From this perspective, the biblical writers were trying for a new beginning, a creation myth that centers God as Yahweh, erasing the long history of Goddess worship before him. And yet, even here, the knowledge of this older world shows up in the serpent, who "tricks" Eve into eating the fruit of the Tree of Knowledge. As a result, Eve learns, perhaps, there is more to life than God.

Some believe that the Tree of Knowledge was a sycamore fig, an ancient symbol of the Goddess. If this is so, Eve eating from this tree meant she was tasting the knowledge of the Goddess, which included knowledge of sexuality, the great secret of creating life. This could give Eve power as well as choice—not ideal in a patriarchal paradise. So perhaps Eve wasn't so stupid after all. Perfection is nice, but it doesn't get us anywhere. We couldn't be the complex, decision-making beings we are without Eve's choice to leave the garden for a world where knowledge, change, and maturity become possible.

EVE: THE TEMPTATION OF KNOWLEDGE

Eve's energy shows up in our lives when we are given the choice between the status quo and the unknown. Eve chooses to eat the fruit, to leap off the cliff, to taste what could be possible outside of what she knows. She transitions from innocent Maiden to creative, powerful Mother.

Take a good look at the status quo in your life. Is this really how you want to live? Forever? Is it worth taking the leap of faith into change? Are you ready—and do you really want—to know?

MEDITATION WITH EVE:

The leap (out) of faith

Prepare for your meditation in a comfortable seat. Set your circle and acknowledge the land. If you'd like, you can journal with these questions as you consider them.

Think of a choice you are facing. Separate the choice into two options: staying the same or changing.

What would it mean to stay the same? Sit with that image for a little while. In a year, five years, ten years, if you stay the same, what does your life look like? How does this image feel in your body?

Now consider changing. If you made a choice that would shift you out of the status quo, what would that look like? Imagine a year, five years, ten years from now. You may only see the unknown—sit with that as well, the feeling of not knowing in your body and how that may feel different from the known.

When you're ready, call up the image of the empowered Eve. See her risking everything she knows to make a change, to learn, to experience the unknown. If you'd like, imagine having a conversation with her. Ask her questions. Listen to her wisdom.

When you're ready, take a deep breath. Thank the circle, the land, your heart, and Eve, honoring her wisdom and her sacred desire to know.

WARRIOR

The Warrior is not a traditional part of the three phases of the goddess cycle, but she's been present as a goddess archetype for a very long time. There are divine feminine Warriors who fight with weather, with nature, with telling the truth, or a lie, with armies, dancing, storytelling, potions, swords, sticks, and fingernails. Her weapons can be subtler than a fist or blunt as a hammer. Ultimately, the Warrior stands up for the sovereign self. She stands alone, but can also stand with the Maiden, Mother, or Crone. The Warrior archetype is present in the waxing moon, the early days of spring, the blood harvest of the late fall, and whenever else she is needed to fight the good fight.

THE MORRÍGAN SISTERS' REVENGE

It was early April. The rivers were flowing, having finally loosened from the grip of the winter's ice. The three sisters stood at the shallow end of the ford, washing their clothes and skin of the blood and gore from their latest battle. Badb, the Banshee, drank deeply of the cool river water, soothing her throat from her screams and wails portending death. Macha, Goddess of the Plain, sprinkled the water of life over her body, shifting, as she does, from death to life and back again, having sacrificed herself defending the land. The Morrígan, Queen of Nightmares, washed the blood from her eye after it was slashed by a prideful hero who didn't understand she was trying to help him. The water gently called her eye back to wholeness, and she could again see beyond seeing. If you blinked, you would see a single woman, an old hag doing the simple work of washing. If you blinked again, you'd see a beautiful woman with red hair and blood-red lips bathing in the river. Blink one more time and you would see a murder of crows settling on the water, their iridescent black feathers shimmering.

"Beltane is coming," said the Badb. "The land needs new birth. Shall we touch the human world again?"

Macha sighed. "If we must," she said, then smiled. The three women pressed their heads gently together, having some silent conversation heard only by them.

They parted, and the Morrígan turned her eye to Macha, knowing she would be the one to go. She showed her an image of a lonely widower, a quiet cattle farmer who was kind to his cows. "We will be with you," the Morrígan told her, and the three women became one again, young and beautiful.

Macha stepped lightly onto the widower Cruinniuc's farm, nodding to the cows and lightly caressing the sheep as she did. In the wallow of each of her footsteps, the green grass grew greener. She entered Cruinniuc's little home and sat down by the hearth as if she'd always been there. When Cruinniuc returned, he found a beautiful woman in the role of his wife. He had been alone for so long he'd forgotten what it was like to have someone waiting for him, someone warm and kind, the smell of food in the house. He sat down next to her and Macha took his hand.

"You will take me as your wife now," she said gently. The man only nodded, knowing better than to question a gift from the faery world.

For years, the couple lived happily. The cows thrived and the hens grew fat and healthy. Cruinnuic became even wealthier, enjoying the gifts of his magical wife. From time to time he would watch her with the animals, seeming to appear in one part of the land and then reappear in another. She would bring forth the creamiest, most delicious milk from the cows, the softest fleece from the sheep, the brightest corn from the fields. She seemed to float in her work, never struggling, never breaking a sweat. He loved and admired his magical wife, wondering what he had done to deserve her.

In time, Macha became pregnant with twins. As she grew close to the time of giving birth, a fair came to the town that Cruinniuc wanted to attend. He was anxious to show off his wealth and happiness since Macha had come into his life.

"You may go, my love, but you must not talk about me at the fair," Macha warned him.

Cruinniuc only nodded, half listening, forgetting that the faery world takes as easily as it gives.

So it was that the town gathered at the fair to watch the king of Ulster's great horse race. As expected, the king's two fastest horses won the race. The bards sang out, "There is not a swifter pair of horses in all of Ireland!"

Without thinking, Cruinniuc burst out, "None faster than my wife!"

The king heard this boast and sent his men to seize the man who'd spoken it. "You will prove your boast or die," he announced.

"My king, I apologize, I spoke out of turn," Cruinniuc protested, realizing all too late that he had made a fatal mistake.

"Bring her here and race her," the King insisted. Despite Cruinniuc's desperate attempts to backtrack, he found himself imprisoned and forced on pain of death to take the king's men to his farm to find her.

When they arrived, Macha had already begun to feel the first pangs of childbirth. The men told her she must race the king's horses. "I cannot," she said. "Do you not see that I am close to giving birth?"

They did see, but told her, "If you do not come, your husband will be killed by the king's decree."

Macha was angry, but she had come to love her husband in the years they'd spent together. She was here to bring life into the world, not to take it away. She knew she must go and allow Cruinniuc to understand the consequences of his actions. The cycle that had begun must end.

She went with the king's men to the fair and was placed at the starting line beside the king's horses. She appealed to the crowd, "Do not make me do this. My birthing pains have begun. It is not right that I be put on display in this condition." She looked to the crowd, trying to find a compassionate face, but they were in the fury of competition and excitement. "I cannot do this!" She cried.

"Unsheathe your swords and put the farmer to death," said the king coldly.

"Wait!" cried Macha. She looked to the crowd again. "Each of you was born to a mother. Please let me give birth before I attempt this task." The people only jeered, insisting on the spectacle. The king had no pity at all.

Macha's eyes hardened, reflecting the Badb behind them, the wail of coming death beginning to hum at the back of her mouth. She felt the Morrígan's warlike arms holding her, readying her for right revenge. "I am Macha, daughter of Sainreth Mac Imbaith, the Strange Son of Ocean. Because you have shown me no mercy, disaster will fall upon you all. My name will forever remain on this place where we stand today. Let us begin."

The crowd cheered and the horse race began. True to her and Cruinniuc's word, she reached the finish line long before the king's horses, but not without pain. She cried out at the finish line and gave birth to her twins, a son and a daughter.

"You have disrespected me. You have forgotten who I am. I shall not protect you and your unworthy king's land," Macha spat. "I curse the men of Ulster for nine generations to be overcome with the pains of childbirth in the time of greatest need. You shall remember me when you are unable to protect this land." The crowd watched in horror as Macha died, her face flashing between herself and her sisters, fierce warrior, old hag, rage of hail and wind and snow, and finally a raven, who cast its eye on each of the bystanders who had let her die that day. Then she flew away.

Ever since that day, the place where Macha gave birth was known as Emain Macha, the Twins of Macha. While Cruinniuc, twice a widower now, forever had to live with what he had done that day, the men of Ulster would suffer Macha's pain and vengeance anytime they tried to take up arms to protect themselves and their land. Whether the unworthy king had learned his lesson or not, his people would be helpless against invasion. The Morrígan sisters had made their mark on the land forever.

THE MORRÍGAN SISTERS: GODDESSES OF THE LAND

The Morrígan sisters, or the *Morrígna*, are Badb, Macha, and the Morrígan, who was also sometimes called Morrígu, Danu, or Nemain. They are sometimes understood as one goddess and sometimes three, representing the triple deity motif seen frequently in mythology to represent different facets of the same concept. The Morrígan came to be in the Celtic era, which began around 1200 BCE and spanned Ireland, the British Isles, northern Italy, Switzerland, France, and parts of Turkey and Poland at its peak. The Celts were mostly defeated by the Romans around the first century CE, and because they generally did not keep written records, most of the sources we have about them were written by their enemies. The most coherent mythological texts were written down by Christian monks in the twelth century CE. We can gather information from these sources, but in many ways this ancient culture remains a mystery.

The Morrígan sisters are a part of the Tuatha Dé Danann, a magical race of people, gods, or faeries. They are said to have arrived in Ireland on "ships from the sky, granting the country great gifts of civilization," as Courtney Weber tells it in her book *The Morrígan*. Sometimes when a new people arrive mysteriously on ships in mythology, it represents a historical arrival of a new, unfamiliar people. These accounts could have been told either by the invaders, seeing themselves as godlike colonizers, or those invaded, having to sort through the reality of a new race of people in their midst. In the stories, the Tuatha Dé Danann interacted with the humans in various ways, sometimes helpful, sometimes not so much. When they were eventually defeated, the Tuatha Dé Danann retreated into the Otherworld, also known as the *sídh* (pronounced *shee*) a world between worlds. The Morrígan sisters are often seen at rivers, fords, and the edges of the water—those liminal places where the earth and the water meet and where the veils between our world and the sídh may be thinner.

The Morrígan sisters are strange goddesses, sometimes benevolent and beautiful, other times terrifying. They are warriors, protecting the land and avenging those who mistreat it, but they can also be mothers, like Macha, bringing life to the land. The Morrígan could be a personification of the land itself, which gives as much as it takes away. Weather was a major factor in whether a battle would be won or lost, and that was everything to a people who did not have a central authority but rather organized into separate groups of ad hoc kingdoms that would spend much of their time battling over land and cattle.

The ancient Celts may have believed that a king's most important role was to be a good "husband" to the land. If the land was happy, it would protect and sustain the people. If not, it could spell disaster. The Ulstermen are punished severely for their king's lack of empathy and respect for (what he thought was) human suffering, and thus forgetting the power of the land. The moral of this story, among other things, is to be careful not to get on the wrong side of the Morrígan.

GODDESS OF SOVEREIGNTY

The Morrígan's resistance is all about knowing who she is. The sisters never carry swords or other traditional weapons of battle. They wail and scream, become a torrent of blood and wind, turn into animals that cause the warriors to trip in their attempts to defend themselves and their land. When men disdain their power because they are women, they laugh and curse these men in ways the men could never have imagined. If the people are respectful and care for the land, the Morrígan can be kind, even generous. But if they dare forget her power and sovereignty, they'd better watch out.

In this story, Macha sees that these people do not deserve the abundance and wellbeing that comes with her peaceful presence, and she withdraws. She not only leaves Cruinniuc poor, suddenly a single father, but she curses the men of this region with the pains of childbirth—an interesting twist on Eve's curse. She not only takes their power away, she makes them feel what she feels. She dies, reverting to her form as goddess, knowing she can return again when she wishes. She forces empathy on them for nine generations. Now that's a curse.

The Morrígan is not the sort of goddess you pray to when you're looking for sweetness and light. She's the goddess you pray to when sweetness and light have left you. As I read about how the Morrígan will tend to appear when you need her, whether you've asked for her or not, I felt a chill run up my spine. As I left behind the first chapters of this book, which are all about new life, potential, and hope, and turned my attention to the fierce Morrígan sisters, death reappeared in my life. With it came a fresh well of grief and hopelessness. But the lessons of the Morrígan are all about sovereignty, even and especially when we are facing the darkest aspects of life. This dark goddess reminded me that, even in my most hopeless moments, I still have choices. I can still be who I am, no matter how oppressed I may feel by factors beyond my control. Weber writes:

> "Tough times call for tough goddesses. Many of the things that will happen to us may be out of our control. The Morrígan is a goddess of many things, but perhaps the greatest one is that of navigating the darkness, and acknowledging our fears and proceeding anyway. Because she walks in the liminal places, she can accompany us through these difficult transitions. The sisters may not solve things for us, but we will not be alone while we try to solve them."

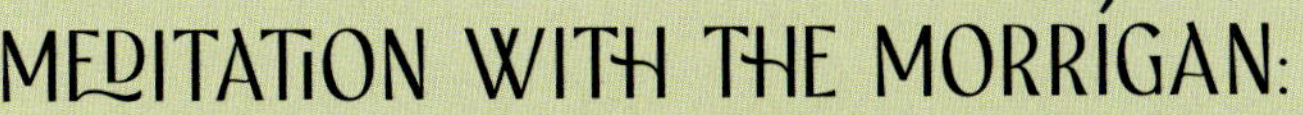

MEDITATION WITH THE MORRÍGAN:

Sovereignty

In this meditation, we will explore feelings of darkness, frustration, or helplessness. You can do this anytime those feelings feel present for you. You may like to light a candle and have a journal nearby.

Find a comfortable position for your meditation. Set your protective circle. Acknowledge the land you are on, and take some extra time here to consider your relationship with this land: how you experience it; how you respect it, or how you don't.

When you're ready, turn your thoughts to your feelings of darkness, helplessness, hopelessness, frustration, or injustice. Notice the feeling in your body and the thoughts that come along with it. Try to stay with the feeling, even if your system might want to distract or numb you away from it.

Imagine the Morrígan is joining you in your circle. She can be Badb, the Banshee, wailing and keening with you in your grief. She can be the Morrígan, a beautiful red-haired warrior ready to fight for what's right. And she can be Macha, who knows the wisdom of death and life and how they are connected. See if one particular version of this goddess resonates most with you right now. It could be all three.

Let the Morrígan witness you in your pain and frustration. Share it with her and let her help you hold it and feel it. Then let her tell you about how there is power in continuing to be yourself, to stand up for yourself and for what's right. Let her help you consider your choices and what it could mean to maintain your sovereignty even in the face of this darkness.

When this feels complete, blow out the candle and close your circle.

LILITH'S REBELLION

Lilith was the Night Bird, the Screech Owl, the Dark Moon. The Hand of Inanna. And then, one day, she was woman, human, set down in the garden of some God she'd never heard of, placed next to a man, both of their bodies made from dust and clay. This man, Adam, told her he was made of good earth, and she was made of dirt. This didn't sound quite right to her, as she knew that dirt and good earth were the same thing, but Adam seemed to believe it.

This God himself had said that he had made them equal. "Let us make man in our image, after our likeness, male and female," he'd said. Lilith was pretty sure she was the female, as she'd always been, but never so soft and naked as this human woman. She didn't dislike it, though, and found the garden to be quite beautiful, full of the fruits and flowers she'd known from the life she'd had before. There was a great sycamore fig here, the Goddess's tree, heavy with the fruits whose taste she remembered, so sweet and soft on her tongue. Here it was called the Tree of Knowledge.

Lilith missed the serpents, though. She was used to seeing them everywhere, on the temples, on the sacred idols, darting in and out of the bushes. She wondered idly where they'd gone as she nibbled the sweet figs and talked with Adam, who was something of a friend and someone to tend the garden with. They'd make love from time to time, and Lilith would take her pleasure in the sacred act of union in her new temple, the garden of this new God.

But one day Adam got frustrated with her in their lovemaking. He told her to lie down in the dirt where she belonged so that he could get on top of her, as God intended.

"And how would you know what God intended, Adam?"

"I know because I am a male, like Him."

"And I am a female, like Him, remember, Adam? Why should I lie beneath you when I am your equal?"

"Well I shall not be the one to lie in the dirt. I am above you, therefore I must be above you."

Lilith laughed, knowing this was not the way. But Adam did not laugh. Lilith's face darkened. A chill of fear passed over her naked skin. She knew all at once that was not the place for her. She knew she was equal to Adam and would not be treated as if she was any less. She remembered the world where the Goddess was supreme, when kings were given their powers only by her grace, when images of the female body were worshiped in the temples. Where making love was a sacred act of honor to the Goddess and the fertility of the land. She did not understand this strange place and she did not like it.

But that was alright, because Lilith knew something Adam did not. The true name of God. Lilith shrieked this secret name, took the form of a screech owl, and flew into the sky. She retreated to the Red Sea, looking for her old home, her old life, where Inanna was Queen of Heaven and Earth and the temples were home and safety. But there was nothing there but wide, shallow sea. She searched and searched, but her home was gone, a wide, depthless nothing in its place.

Lilith cried, her tears salting the sea, until she found others who had been exiled, like her, who remembered the world of the Goddess, others whom she learned had been named demons. She found comfort in these others, trying in vain to recreate the beautiful world she'd known before. So God's people called her demon, too, called her children demon, said she flew around at night trying to steal the babies of God's children. She became a monster to them. But Lilith didn't care. She stayed in this night world, far away from God and his counterfeit garden. Her home was gone. But Lilith was free.

LILITH THE DEMON(IZED)

The name Lilith appears very early on, dating back to about 2100 BCE with the first tablets of the *Epic of Gilgamesh*, where she is referred to as the Hand of Inanna. This likely references the role of the priestess who would call men into the temple to perform the sexual rites known as the sacred marriage. It's speculated that during this time, these temple priestesses would choose the men they wanted to perform these sexual rites with, and that any children born from this union would have been raised by the temple, the community, and/or their mothers. It wouldn't have mattered who the father was because these were matriarchal and matrilineal societies where women held power.

Of course, this could be something of a wistful feminist reading. We would love to think there was a time when women had more power, where sex was always sacred and consensual, and children would have been welcomed and raised by the community. The truth is we really don't know.

We do know, however, that there was a major clash in worldviews between these likely matriarchal Goddess worshippers and the believers in a male God represented by the Hebrew Bible. As Merlin Stone convincingly argues in her book *When God Was a Woman*, the writers and editors of the Old Testament were working in the lineage of invading cultures that brought patriarchal thought into the indigenous matriarchies. Their God was male and their children held their father's name. In order to control reproduction and ensure paternity was known, these patriarchal authorities needed to essentially teach women sexual shame. This would, of course, have put the temple priestesses out of a job.

Several books of the Old Testament detail a "holy war" against the people, usually named Canaanites, who worshiped the goddess Ashtoreth (or Asherah) and her consort Baal. The name Ashtoreth is also sometimes written as Astarte, and is likely a version of Ishtar, a later name for Inanna. Stone quotes one particularly alarming passage in Deuteronomy:

> "When you wage war against your enemy and the Lord your God delivers them into your hands and you take some of them captive; then if you see a comely woman among the captives and take a liking to her, you may marry her. You shall bring her into your house, where she shall shave her head, pare her nails, and discard the clothes she had when she was captured. Then she shall stay in your house and mourn her father and mother for a full month. After that you may have intercourse with her; you shall be her husband and she your wife." (Deuteronomy 21:10–14)

This is one example of many times throughout history that one culture has overtaken another, often by murdering all the men and raping or "marrying" the women. These women may have been forced to convert to a new religion, but they don't forget their old ways. In this sense, Lilith's story could be one of those ways—a kind of rebel remembering that was folded into biblical mythology.

Lilith is not named explicitly in the canonical biblical creation stories, but she appears in Hebrew mythology and folklore as a way to explain the difference between the first two creation myths in the Bible. The first story reads that "God created mankind in his own image, in the image of God he created them, male and female he

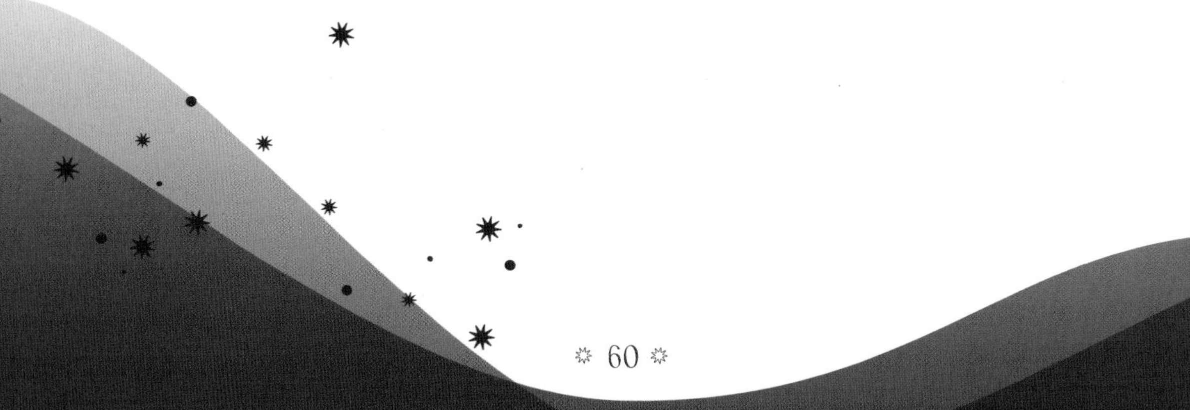

created them" (Genesis 1:27). A few pages later, we read about Adam alone in the garden and God creating Eve from his rib. The story goes that Lilith was the woman in this first story, but she didn't like Adam's request that she lay underneath him when they made love. She argued that they were, indeed, equal, and Adam disagreed. So Lilith uttered the secret name of God and flew out to the Red Sea, where she bred with thousands of demons, creating demon babies at a startling rate. God sent angels to try to get her back, and in some versions, God threatened to kill 100 of her children every day until she returned. She still refused, so God was forced to try again, this time with Eve.

Lilith was, in a sense, the first witch, the first woman to be seen as evil because she believed in her own power. Like the witches who were burned in the early modern era in Europe and North America, Lilith was accused of eating babies and having sex with the Devil. Most of the witches who were tortured and killed in the witch hunting era, which lasted from about the 1400s to the 1800s CE, were women who had some sort of sexual agency that represented a threat to the patriarchal and capitalist authorities at the time. They were often midwives, herbalists, or healers who knew something about contraception and abortion. They were widows without an interest in remarrying. They were demonized, just like Lilith, for daring to hold knowings that were not officially sanctioned by the Church authorities at the time.

LILITH THE REBEL

Lilith may be an exile, a demon, and a monster, but she won't play by anyone's rules but her own. She would rather live at the edge of society as herself than fit in as someone else. She is an embodiment of the power of righteous rage, the anger of injustice that arises when you know something is wrong and you have to do something about it, no matter what the consequences may be. To this day, Lilith's name is invoked as a symbol of feminist resistance. Lilith is our activist ancestor.

Some Warriors are subtle, working within the system to create change. While that can be incredibly important, Lilith is a different kind of Warrior. She's the one who stands up for what she believes in no matter what people think of her. She'd rather quit than be forced to play a game rigged for her to lose. She may have made it this far in the guise of a demon, but we can see her true face. Lilith is a goddess of divine rebellion.

MEDITATION WITH LILITH:

The power of anger

This meditation will explore the power of working with your anger. Set your circle and acknowledge the land that you are on. Light your candle if you are using one and have a journal nearby if you wish. When you're ready, invite the energy of your anger. Feel it in your body. Notice its texture, movement, shape, energy, and where you feel it. For many of us, anger feels like a spark or flame in the solar plexus. It sometimes gets caught in the jaw where we feel we can't speak our truth or ask for what we need. Try to relax your jaw muscles and imagine allowing the anger to flow.

If anger could speak for itself, what would it say?

What injustice does it see?
What need is not being met?
What boundary is being crossed?
What values are being threatened?
Whose power or voice is at risk?

Invite Lilith to join you in this meditation. See her flying free, powerful, knowing herself clearly and joyfully. Let her remind you of your powers in this moment. Listen to her wisdom, her truth. Let it speak to the spark of anger within you. Anger is most powerful when it is clearly articulated with a strong and unshakable sense of boundaries, needs, and values. Consider what you're willing to sacrifice to right the wrongs that have been done. Remember that any actions you take should be in alignment with your integrity, your values, and the highest good of all.

When this feels complete, thank the circle, Lilith, the land, and your anger for speaking your righteous truth.

MEDUSA'S GREAT BEAUTY

Medusa was born in the sea and of it. Her mother, Ceto, was a goddess of sea creatures, especially the whales, sharks, and other giants of the water, and her father, Phorkys, was half god and half fish. Medusa had many siblings, all monsters, many terrifying, all immortal.

But Medusa was different. She was almost super-humanly beautiful, with high cheekbones, a long nose, and creamy golden skin. Her thick, black hair fell over her shoulders in soft ample curls, and her lips were the velvety red of a poppy. She was the only mortal of all her siblings.

So Medusa spent her time on land with humans—mortals, just like her. She loved Athena, a goddess of wisdom who consorted with no other god. Medusa became a priestess in her temple, spending all her time there, day and night, worshiping the virgin goddess.

One day Poseidon, a god of the sea and storms, noticed Medusa and her striking beauty. He approached her at the temple, wanting to get closer to her beauty, to hold it in his hands. Medusa knew that Athena was against consorting with any male, whether god or human. And yet she did find Poseidon alluring. He reminded her of her home in the ocean. She let him approach her, curious as to what he'd say.

"Lie with me, Medusa. I want to touch your beauty, to hold you in my hands, possess you for myself."

Medusa shook her head. "The act of love is not a possession. It is a sacred act of creation and honor to the goddess. Are you here in worship or in wanting?"

"I will worship you, Medusa, if that is what you want." Poseidon stepped closer, his eyes narrowing.

"I do not, Poseidon. I worship Athena here, where the goddess is supreme. I would serve her and make her children if she wanted that, but she does not and I do not. Leave here and do not come back."

As Medusa turned her beautiful face away from Poseidon, he grabbed her hand and overpowered her, taking her for his own reasons, defiling the sacredness of the sexual act and of the temple. Medusa cried out for help, and Athena herself appeared, just in time to witness the sacrilege, happening on her very altar.

Furious, Athena held up her shield and screamed a deep, guttural cry of betrayal and grief. She pointed her sword at Poseidon's heart, knowing she could not kill him, but that didn't mean she wouldn't try. Seeing the trouble he was in, he dissolved into a weak puddle, sliding back into the ocean unscathed, unpunished.

Medusa found herself and her beloved goddess alone at the desecrated altar. She began to cry, great drops of ocean streaming down her face. Athena straightened her priestess's torn tunic and brushed the tears from her perfect cheeks.

"My child," she spoke, barely containing her fury. "We maintain our power here as virgins. We cannot give our power to any male, god nor human. What have you done?"

Medusa was silent, tears filling her eyes and mouth, her jaw tight. Athena softened, understanding.

"I cannot punish Poseidon. The gods have taken more power than they should have and they would take his side. I cannot make this wrong right. What am I to do?"

The two women sat in silence for a moment. At last Medusa opened her poppy-red lips. "Make me a monster," she said simply, thinking of her sisters, safely tucked away in a cave near the Hesperides. "Make me horrifying so that no man will ever want me again. Make me look the way I feel inside, violated, half dead, filled with the rage of having lost what I cannot get back." Athena looked at her priestess, her beautiful face already tightening with shame and betrayal.

"Place the serpents of the Great Goddess on my head and her golden wings on my back," Medusa continued, her rage beginning to glow behind her eyes, drying her tears with its heat. "But make me so repulsive that anyone who sees me will die of the shame of having made the Goddess into a monster."

Athena set her jaw and nodded. With that, Medusa's long luscious hair turned into a mass of hissing vipers. Her golden skin turned a pale shade of green, fangs grew out of her teeth and her eyes turned black with the rage she felt inside. Medusa was a dark mirror of the old Athena, the serpent goddess from before the gods came and inserted themselves into her land, forcing Athena to become a Warrior.

"Go now, my child," said the goddess, "Be free from men and their tyranny. I will always be with you."

Medusa fled on her golden wings to the lonely cave near the Hesperides with her sisters, the Gorgons, who reveled in their hideousness at the edge of the world. When Medusa wandered alone in the blistering sun, birds grew still and fell from the sky. Beasts passing by would see her and instantly become one of the rocks. From time to time, heroes would come with the task of killing the mortal Medusa, but as soon as they saw her, they were paralyzed, swords raised uselessly forever. No living creature could bear to look at her face. Not even the serpents on her head.

Every time a being turned to stone, Medusa felt the revenge of the wrongs done to her and her goddess on the altar. She felt the rage of the vipers who were once honored, now feared, banished to dark caves by the gods who did not understand them. Over and over, she watched living beings dying of the shame of what had been done to her and her goddess.

But Medusa knew they didn't really understand. The beasts and birds and heroes were petrified too quickly to take in what they were seeing, to feel the pain she wanted them to feel at what had been done to her. She wandered alone, punishing and punished. She yearned for the day someone could make it close enough to end her misery, but no one ever had.

Until, at last, Perseus appeared at the cave. As this one entered, Medusa saw the glint of something familiar—her goddess Athena's shield, shimmering in the light like a mirror. Her goddess had returned to her at last, hearing her prayers to end her miserable existence. As soon as she saw Perseus's face in his glimmering shield, his sword freed her head from her body, sending the mortal Medusa's soul to rest.

Medusa's head, however, maintained its power to turn anyone who saw it to stone. As it decayed and rotted, it became all the more terrifying, and Perseus continued to use it to fight for justice on behalf of the great Athena. When Perseus finally brought her priestess's head to her as a tribute, Athena immortalized Medusa on her own shield, forever carrying the memory of the snake-headed priestess into the battles she fought every day.

MEDUSA: THE SERPENT-HAIRED SEA MONSTER

Medusa is best known for her role in the hero Perseus's story, where he collects her serpent-infested head with the goddess Athena's help and turns his enemies into stone with the power of its ugliness. This story is a part of the classical Greek mythological canon, mostly written down by Homer and Hesiod in the seventh century BCE. The Roman poet Ovid, writing around the first century, filled in some details about Medusa's backstory, namely that she was born beautiful and that Athena cursed her with a head of vipers after Poseidon raped her in Athena's temple.

And yet there is a layer to this story that goes back much farther in ancient history: Athena was once a serpent goddess.

In her book *Lost Goddesses of Early Greece*, Charlene Spretnak explains that goddess worship was present long before invaders from the north brought the concept of Zeus and the male gods around 2500 BCE. Before this patriarchal people inserted themselves into the indigenous goddess culture, Athena was often shown with a crown of serpents on her head and adorning her robe, holding another serpent gently in her hand. In this form, she likely had a relationship with fertility and the land. Now, she is most frequently shown as a cold warlike goddess, protectress of the city, wearing a winged helmet and armor.

The serpent was once the most common symbol of the Goddess. Because they shed their skins, they represent death and rebirth, the Goddess's cycle, just as the uterus sheds and regrows its lining each month. By the time the serpent shows up in Eve's garden, it was already demonized by those who wanted to suppress the Goddess and her symbols.

Athena herself had a strange birth: she emerged, fully formed, from her father Zeus's head. Her mother, Metis, was a goddess of wisdom who had become pregnant by Zeus. But he knew there was a prophecy that warned that if this child was born, it would take over his power and primacy as god of the gods. So Zeus swallowed Metis whole. Athena still found a way out, though, up through the head instead of down through the womb. Anne Baring and Jules Cashford point out in their book *The Myth of the Goddess* that "the swallowing of the pregnant mother and birth through the head of the father has the same uneasy dissonance as does the birth of Eve from Adam's rib."

Athena's birth from Zeus's head is a strong shift away from the primacy of the power of the womb, a central aspect of the ancient Goddess, and toward an age where intelligence and rationality became associated with masculinity. At the same time, however, it is a nod to parthenogenesis, the ability to create life without sexual reproduction. The word literally means "virgin birth" and is related to Athena Parthenos, the virgin goddess who is powerful on her own, without a man, and whose temple, the Parthenon, still stands in Greece today. Before humans understood how babies were made, it appeared that women created life from nothing—parthenogenetically. Thus, obviously, god was a woman. Until, of course, men showed up capable of giving birth from their heads.

From this perspective, maybe Athena didn't curse Medusa, but rather gifted her with a crown of serpents just like hers used to be, in the era before the patriarchal gods took over. She may have needed to take on the form of cold, unfeeling Warrior in order to survive and stay relevant in a world overwritten by the invaders. But her ancient form as serpent goddess was not lost. The goddess has had to go underground so many times throughout history, shedding her old skins and growing new ones to stay present and powerful, even if that sometimes meant becoming monstrous. Like Lilith, Medusa represents a kind of rebel remembering, a version of Athena in her pre-patriarchal form. Even in her form as patriarchal Warrior goddess, Athena immortalizes Medusa on her shield forever, a symbol of coded resistance in a patriarchal world.

THE POWER OF UGLINESS

Medusa was wronged in so many ways, and, to this day, she shows up as a monster in many a hero's story. She was raped by a male god on the altar of her beloved goddess. She does not even survive her own story. And yet she resists. She resists by insisting on showing the ugliness of what Poseidon did—and, perhaps, what was done to the goddess's worshippers by the northern invaders—on her own face.

Many survivors of trauma feel a great shame about what was done to them. No matter what happened (or didn't), survivors tend to feel that something is wrong with them, that what happened to them has turned them ugly, shameful, too horrible to be seen. That shame freezes us—it can make us go numb, turning our gazes away in avoidance. These traumas, however, often have a relationship with larger oppressive systems, like patriarchy, capitalism, and white supremacy, that we can't control. Survivors tend to internalize these injustices, swallowing the oppression with shame and silence. Medusa does not do that. She wears her injustice outwardly. She may not be able to change the outcome of her story, but she refuses to let it disappear in shame and silence. Her ugliness is also truth.

In order to heal ourselves, we need to unfreeze that shame. We need to witness our own inner ugliness, the parts of ourselves that were violated, taken advantage of, or made powerless, melting these parts with the gaze of compassion. If we are willing to be honest enough with ourselves to meet our inner Medusas, if we can witness the horrors and keep breathing, we can begin to claim back our power. We can see the marks of feminine power within us as the serpent that can shed its skin and become new again. Medusa's ugliness sets her free, and she remains powerful even today, thousands of years after her birth and death. Are you willing to look into her eyes?

MEDITATION WITH MEDUSA:

Unfreezing shame

This meditation is about melting shame with compassion.

Set yourself up in front of a mirror and light your candle. Honor and acknowledge the land that you are on and your relationship with this land. Consider Medusa's land and your relationship with that part of the world and its stories. Honor all we can't know, all that has been swallowed up by time. Call up your protective circle.

Now consider something that you find ugly within yourself. This could be something you dislike about the way you look, but it could also be a moment in time, a feeling you have, a quality within yourself that you're not crazy about. Look into your own eyes as you sit with this quality or feeling. See the truth of that ugliness. Stay with the images, emotions, thoughts, or sensations that come up here. Do your best to simply observe. Keep breathing through it all. Notice shame, if it comes up, which can feel like nausea, panic, or numbness. Keep breathing. Don't look away.

Now look for the power hidden within this ugliness. If it is a part of your body, how does this body part work for you? How does it function to keep you alive? Or how does it tell a story about something you've been through? If it's a behavior, what have you learned from it or how did it help you survive? If it's something that happened to you, how did you survive it?

Invite the energy of compassion into this experience with you. Imagine Medusa sitting with you, witnessing you, understanding deeply what you've been through. Now take a few deep breaths, releasing that experience. Return your attention to the room you're in, the land beneath you. Rub your hands together. Thank the land, the circle, and the energy of Medusa for showing you the truth behind your ugliness.

MOTHER

The Mother archetype is the creatrix, the one who can bring forth life from her mind or her body. She is the fullness of summer, the full moon, the ripe fruit ready to be eaten, the one on the precipice of transformation. She can represent literal motherhood, but she is also about giving forth from her body and her mind, creating beauty, art, relationships, even new worlds from the emptiness of Nothing.

SKYWOMAN: MOTHER OF EARTH

Before the beginning, before there was earth, there was a world of water.

Far above the water was Skyworld, a beautiful place filled with beings who were loving and gentle, who dreamed their wisdom to life. Skyworld was perfect, and everyone loved it there.

But one day, something very unusual happened. A young woman named Iotsitsisen became ill with something no one had ever seen before: curiosity. She would wander the beauty of Skyworld, wondering what was outside of it, what its edges felt like. From time to time she would lay, belly down, her ear to the ground, listening for what might be underneath her perfect world. She wanted to know.

One night in a restless sleep, she dreamed about the Tree of Life, which grew strong in the center of Skyworld. In her dream, there was a great hole underneath the tree. Its darkness was beautiful and inviting. When she awoke, she knew she must go to the tree and discover what was underneath it.

When she arrived at the tree the next morning, she found her husband and her parents there. All three had shared the same dream, and they knew they needed to help Iotsitsisen find what was underneath the Tree of Life. They worked together to scoop the soft earth away from the roots of the tree, and before long they found a giant hole with a deep darkness and something glittering far beneath. Iotsitsisen peered into the hole, her heart and her womb fluttering, knowing that this was exactly where she needed to be.

Iotsitsisen fell easily and simply through the hole, her loved ones watching, worried and afraid but understanding that there was something happening that was beyond what they knew in Skyworld.

Iotsitsisen was not afraid. She felt the wind caressing her hair, the glint of blue water beneath her, the world she had been dreaming about and needing to know rushing up to meet her body.

Far below, many eyes looked up at the shaft of golden light appearing from the sky. As if they were of one mind, a flock of geese took flight immediately to collect the falling person onto their wings, breaking her fall.

The animals of the water far below called together a council. The geese held Skywoman for now, but there was no place for her naked feet to land, and all the animals agreed to help this strange being in distress.

From the great depths of the ocean, Turtle arose and offered his back as a place for the falling woman to rest her feet. She stepped gently from the wings of the geese to the sturdy back of Turtle. She met the eyes of all the animal people who had gathered together to help her even though they didn't know who she was. She touched her heart in gratitude, feeling tears brimming at her eyes. She wondered if they had dreamed about her as she had dreamed about this world beneath her world.

She was steady enough on Turtle's back, but all agreed she would need more room. Some of the water birds had heard that there was earth far below the surface of the water. Perhaps they could bring some up for her to walk upon.

Beaver offered to try first. She took a great breath and dove into the water, swimming down for a long time but finding nothing. At last she floated to the surface, exhausted, her paws empty. Loon dove went next, swimming down with his powerful wings. He, too, was gone for a long time, but arose breathless and exhausted without any mud. Strong swimmers tried, animals who could hold their breath for a long time, but none could bring up the earth.

Muskrat was smaller than the other animals, not as strong or swift. But she was determined. She dove down into the deep, down until all was dark, down until the strange, slow, deep-water fish could watch her with their nearly sightless eyes. Just before she gave in to the heaviness of the water, she scraped the bottom of the ocean, collecting a small amount of mud in her paw.

The other animals thought they had lost Muskrat forever. But at long last, she floated to the surface, her paw clutched around a small amount of earth. Muskrat had given her life to the task, and had succeeded.

Skywoman bent her forehead to the soft lifeless head of the Muskrat, thanking her deeply. She gently opened Muskrat's paw and spread the earth onto Turtle's back with the help of the other animals. She bowed low to them all, especially Muskrat, moved by their generosity, wisdom, and kindness. She began to sing and dance in thanksgiving, her feet connecting to the precious earth.

As she danced and sang, the animals joined her, the magic of their connection creating more and more mud and sand and dirt beneath their feet. Skywoman noticed that there was something clutched in her own hand as well: a handful of seeds and berries that she had grabbed from the Tree of Life as she was falling through the great hole. She opened her hand, allowing the seeds to scatter over the land, creating great trees and abundant plants that could feed the animals. She touched her belly, remembering the unborn child within it, and rejoiced that she would bring this child into a new world created in relationship with these animal people. This world was to become her new home, and it would be named Turtle Island.

SKYWOMAN AND TURTLE ISLAND

Skywoman is a story that is told and retold in many indigenous cultures on Turtle Island, which is now also known as North America. She is especially known to the Haudenosaunee, an alliance that includes the Mohawk, Oneida, Onondaga, Cayuga, Seneca, and Tuscarora people of the region we now call Southern Ontario, Quebec, and New York State; and to the Council of Three Fires, which includes the Ojibwe, Potawatomi, and Odawa peoples of the Great Lakes, upper Mississippi River, and Great Plains regions. These people have likely been on those lands since at least 4000 BCE. These stories are most often shared orally, so details change here and there. The above version was gathered in conversation with those told in *Braiding Sweetgrass* by Robin Wall Kimmerer, a member of the Potawatomi Nation; *Skywoman: Legends of the Iroquois* by Joanne Shenandoah, a member of the Oneida Indian Nation, and Douglas M. George-Kanentiio, a member of the Mohawk Nation; *Native American Stories* by Joseph Bruchac, a member of the Nulhegan Abenaki Nation; and "This is History," an essay by Mohawk writer Beth Brant.

Much like in the Garden of Eden (which is a much, much younger story than this one), there is a Tree of Life on Skyworld. Iotsitsisen, pronounced *Yo-ji-ji-sen*, which means "Mature Flower" (also called Atahensic or Eagentci in other versions) becomes sick (with curiosity, in Beth Brant's version), which is a brand new experience for Skyworld. Dreams are the conduit for wisdom and knowing here, so Skywoman and her family work together to help uproot the Tree of Life and open the portal to the world below.

Eventually, Skywoman gives birth to her daughter, Tekawerahkwa, or "Gusts of Wind" in Shenandoah and George-Kanentiio's story, also sometimes translated as "Earth Woman." This young girl grows up loving her mother's earth but feeling lonely, much like Persephone, with a deep sense that there must be something more for her than tending her mother's good earth. She becomes pregnant by the spirit of the West Wind, but sadly dies giving birth to her two sons.

In *Braiding Sweetgrass*, Kimmerer explains how the heartbroken Skywoman buries her daughter in the earth. But from Tekawerahkwa's body, more gifts arise: the nourishing and medicinal plants that are still sacred to the people. The strawberry grew from Tekawerahkwa's heart, and is known in Potawatomi as *ode min*, the heart berry. Strawberries are usually the first to bear fruit in the summer, and are sometimes called the Mother of all berries. The goddess cycle recurs again: from death comes rebirth.

In her grief, Iotsitsisen places her own head in the sky, becoming Grandmother Moon, looking down on the legacy of her daughter and grandsons, keeping watch and staying present eternally. The rest of her body remains on the earth, providing more gifts, especially corn, beans, and squash. Kimmerer explains that these sacred plants are known as the Three Sisters: "Together these plants—corn, beans, and squash—feed the people, feed the land, and feed our imaginations, telling us how we might live." These plants grow better when they are planted close together and struggle when they are planted alone. They teach us how to work together to create something more than we could as individuals. "In reciprocity," Kimmerer writes, "we fill our spirits as well as our bellies."

SKYWOMAN THE ANCESTOR

I am a white woman living in Canada, which is a part of Turtle Island. My ancestors are from England and Ireland, places I've never lived. I've never experienced the seasons in those places. I was born near Lake Ontario on Haudenosaunee land. I live in the northern prairies now, on Plains Cree land, where I feel the bite of the bitterly cold winters and see the first buds on the apple trees in spring. I grow raspberries in my backyard and watch my three year old pick them gleefully, straight from the vine into his mouth. I used to get lost in the forest outside of my family's cottage in Quebec on Mohawk land, sucking the sweet roots of clover petals and playing in my uncle's apple orchard. My ancestors aren't from here beyond a few generations back, but this is the land I know and love. I want to understand its stories, even and especially because they aren't mine, because it was my ancestral people who tried to silence these stories.

I didn't learn the myths and meanings of the Indigenous land when I was a child. I didn't hear about how people who looked like me wanted this land, intended to steal it, and in so doing, subjugated, oppressed, traumatized, and nearly destroyed the people who were here first. These were the people who shared indispensable knowledge about how to survive in these lands out of friendship with these European visitors, who then went on to betray and nearly eradicate them. While these betrayals happened in generations past (and continue to happen in many ways), the trauma is passed down intergenerationally. We can still see the effects of that trauma today in the form of chronic illness, alcoholism, and disproportionately high rates of incarceration for Indigenous populations.

That trauma didn't come from nowhere. The European settlers weren't leaving Paradise because they were curious. The people who wanted a fresh start in the New World were leaving abject poverty, devastating disease, and high levels of daily brutality within the public theatre of crime and punishment. Rather than learn from the people they encountered on these new lands, tragically, the settlers shared their traumas, inflicting them on a people who could have taught them something about how to heal.

I love Skywoman's story of love and loss, the gifts of a generous mother who creates with a song. But this story isn't about my land. I am an alien here, a settler, a child of colonizers who came from another place. And yet, as Kimmerer points out,

"It is good to remember that the original woman was herself an immigrant. She fell a long way from her home in the Skyworld, leaving behind all who knew her and who held her dear. She could never go back."

My ancestors were also immigrants. My paternal great grandfather George was given up by his parents and sent alone across the ocean to become an indentured servant for a rich family in Quebec. The Home Children project sent more than 100,000 children from England to Australia, New Zealand, South Africa, and Canada beginning in 1869 all the way through to the 1970s. These orphaned children, some as young as six months old, were sent to work for strangers in a new country, never to see their parents again.

George escaped his servitude, found work for himself, and married an Irishwoman named Mary who died shortly after giving birth to their three children, including my grandfather Hugh. "Single father" was barely a concept at that time. If there was any trouble, children would be sent to the orphanage without a second thought. But George decided not to do what was done to him. He kept his children, doing his best to work and keep them fed while the children mostly raised each other.

My family came from Christian England and Ireland, steeped in the mythologies of Eve and Mary. They were taught that their connection with God was not on the land, but somewhere far away in heaven, where God was, and that they would find their answers in the male authorities of the Church. These were the same authorities that were taking indigenous children away from their parents and "civilizing" them in residential schools where they were abused, physically and sexually, while their language, their culture, and their connection with the land was literally beaten out of them. This abandonment and abuse of children was not invented for the indigenous people being colonized. It was the way of the colonizer.

Inflicting the kind of pain on children that was seen in the residential schools is only really possible for those whose empathy has been traumatized out of them. Kimmerer points out, "Look at the legacy of poor Eve's exile from Eden: the land shows the bruises of an abusive relationship. It's not just land that is broken, but more importantly, our relationship to land."

Our traumas are different, to be sure. But we all need healing. Maybe Skywoman with her gifts, the plant teachers, could help show us the way.

SKYWOMAN THE MOTHER

As a mother with a beautiful living child and five soul children who came and left my body in early pregnancy, I relate deeply to Skywoman's story and her grief. My experience of becoming a mother has been about both life and death, joy and loss, deep learning alongside brutal tragedy. I've come to understand that my womb performs a cycle of death and rebirth every month, releasing and then creating a new ground for the possibility of new life. I understand that desire to give my body to my children, to stay with them somehow, even after my death, like Grandmother Moon. I've felt the limitations of my power to create, feeling the risk and loss that can come with hoping for new life.

Skywoman's sickness could only be cured by leaving, by changing to become a new version of herself. That sickness, like Eve, Inanna, and Persephone's deep desire to know, is the push we need to slip through the dark portal into the unknown. Becoming Mother must mean leaving behind Maiden, making the choice to step into a phase of painful knowing and powerful sovereignty where, like Skywoman, we have to invent the very ground beneath our feet.

The earth is our first mother, no matter where we come from. She knows all about life and death, hope and despair, loss and change. No matter what we've done or what we've lost, no matter how far we are from the land of our ancestors, we can still lay down with her on her wide, soft belly. She is so much older and wiser than we could ever be, than any biological mother could be. Skywoman became the eternal Grandmother Moon, that witness who can be with us even when things feel really, really bad. So when you really need your mama, remember the earth beneath your feet. Go outside and touch a tree. Eat the food brought forth from her body, abundant even now, after everything she's been through. Drink deeply of her waters. Love her and care for her. Let your healing heal her wounds, too.

MEDITATION WITH SKYWOMAN:

Honoring the earth

If you can, go outside to be near a tree or some wild strawberries or other food growing from the ground. If you need to be inside, consider having some locally grown food, plants, or flowers with you. Or simply sit near a window or contemplate the natural world. Light a candle if you'd like.

Begin by acknowledging the earth beneath your feet. Consider the names of this land, including indigenous names if possible. Think about your relationship with this land, how you and your ancestors got here, how long your family has been in this place. If your homeland is elsewhere, take some time to think about where you and your ancestors are from. We are all indigenous to somewhere. Imagine and contemplate the land there. Allow any feelings to arise around what happened with your ancestors, what you know about the history of the land where you are.

Come back to the present, and consider the season, the weather, the air, the quality of the light, and the phase of the Moon. The feeling of gravity, of connection to the land and the way it supports your body. Notice your body as an extension of the earth, that you are that which supports you. Feel your physical connection to the earth, the space you take up in your body, the material reality of who you are. Notice the way the earth holds you no matter how long you and your family have been in this particular place. Consider the gifts of the land. Depending on the season, there may be abundant fruits and flowers right now, a season of life, or you might be in a winter or fall season, a time of withdrawal, quiet, and death. Notice that there are gifts either way, of abundance or of quiet. What can you learn from what the earth is teaching you right now?

Sit with these thoughts and feelings as long as you'd like. When this feels complete, offer deep gratitude to the earth, the land, the ancestors of this land, and your own ancestors.

NUT: SKY MOTHER

In the beginning, there was Nun: Nothing. Out of Nothing came Something: an egg. The egg flowed in the primordial waters of Nun until it cracked, and there was Atum, the Beginning. Atum rose from the primordial waters and created Shu, Air, and Tefnut, Moisture. Shu and Tefnut fell in love and gave birth to Geb, Earth, and Nut, Sky.

Nut was beautiful, a wide expanse of limitless darkness. Her arms and legs wrapped around Geb, the wide sand dunes and waters of Earth, who loved her passionately. She gave birth to Ra, the Sun, Khonsu, the Moon, and all the stars, whom she installed in her vast body, caring for them forever. The love between Nut and Geb was so intense, so constant and pure, that Ra became jealous, pushing the Sky away from the Earth, creating Day. Ra tasked his grandfather, Shu, with holding the two apart. But at night, Shu rested, exhausted from his labors, and the darkness settled over the Earth again. Nut and Geb continued their love story for millennia, creating the countless constellations of the night sky.

Ra allowed this, as he loved to stare at his mother at night and no one questioned his authority during the day. He loved her sparkling skin, the endless flow of milky stars, the giant planets that would roll and spin across the expanse of everything. Ra created Thoth, god of wisdom, to help him admire the movements of the sky, understand time, and study the intricacies of his mother's body. But this peaceful rhythm was not to last. Geb wanted his own children, too, Earth children who would walk on his sandy ground, explore his caves and rivers, and create their own children on his body.

So it was that Nut became pregnant again, this time with five children who were different from all the others. These would not become planets or pinpricks of light. They would walk upon the Earth as Geb had wanted. They would have powers, different from those of Ra, powers that had never been seen before. As they brewed in Nut's belly, she waited with hopeful anticipation to meet them. She began to shine differently, her body stretching out like a river of sparkling milk, ripe with these strange new children. When Ra discovered this, he became fearful and angry, worried these new beings would threaten the world he had come to think of as his. He cursed Nut so that she would be unable to give birth on any of the 360 days of his solar year.

Nut was becoming uncomfortably full with her children and wanted to be able to bring them to light as she had done so many times before. She was unwilling to let her son Ra dictate whether or not she could do this thing she had done so easily since the beginning of time. She knew he was a difficult one to argue with, however, so she decided instead to ask for help from Ra's favorite child, Thoth.

Thoth adored Nut like everyone else. She was unbearably beautiful, wise, constant, and kind. She had never been cruel or dismissive, but only held them all with an unconditional love that was as boundless as the black edges of her own endless body. Thoth immediately agreed to help Nut give birth to her children, and he came up with a plan.

Thoth knew Khonsu, the Moon, loved a good gamble. At that time, Khonsu was almost as bright as Ra himself, and Thoth knew he had a little light to spare. So he challenged Khonsu to a game of dice. If Thoth won, the agreement went, he would take just a little bit of the Moon's light for himself.

Khonsu couldn't resist a wager, so the two played and played, with Thoth taking little bits of the Moon's light with him every time he won. Nut's labors increased as she waited, hoping for a miracle, until Thoth at last came through. He had collected enough moonlight to add five more days to the solar year, days that would be outside of Ra's control. The Moon was significantly diminished by the time the games were finished, but Khonsu knew that all's fair in dice, and was happy to help his Mother, too, as he loved her as much as Thoth did.

So it was that Nut gave birth to her Earth children at last. On each of these five days came Osiris, god of the afterlife; Isis, goddess of magic; Set, god of storms; Nephthys, goddess of darkness; and Horus, god of truth.

These gods created a new way of being on Geb, raising temples, hosting ceremonies and celebrations, creating a new race of people who would worship them and learn from them about the sky and the cycles of life and death on Earth. Every year, the people celebrated these five days, honoring the Mother that allowed the gods, and thus the people, to be born.

Through the rise and fall of many kings, pharaohs, and other leaders, even those who named the night sky differently and forgot her stories, Nut remains to this day. She embraces the Earth and her many generations of children with clear and limitless love. Whoever they are, wherever they come from, whatever mistakes they might have made, she draws them all back into her darkness when it is their time, installing them into her body as stars forever.

NUT: WOMB TO TOMB

Nut (pronounced "noot") is a beloved ancient Egyptian deity who dates back to prehistoric Egypt (circa 3100 BCE). *The Book of Nut*, which was likely written around 1800 BCE, was an ancient astrological text exploring the sky, the stars, the movement of the Sun, and ways of understanding time by observing the constellations.

A common story about Nut is that she swallows Ra, god of the Sun, every evening and gives birth to him again every morning. Some believe she represents the Milky Way, which looks like a woman (if you squint). From this view, she swallows Ra every spring equinox and births him again at the winter solstice. The five extra days said to have been created by Thoth are called epagomenal or intercalary days that shifted the calendar year from 360 to 365 days, and were celebrated every year.

While deity worship was often more focused on Isis, Horus, or Ra in different time periods, Nut was always the one to come home to. Her image is everywhere in tombs and coffins, either as a starry sky on the ceiling of the tomb or as a beautiful woman with wings outstretched, ready to receive the dead back to their Mother's breast. She was drawn both on the outside of coffins, as if to show the spirit where to go after death, and on the inside of the coffin lid, as if to reassure the dead that they were going home.

NUT: THE ULTIMATE MOTHER

Nut is often depicted as a naked woman whose skin is dark, glittering with stars. She stretches over the Earth, her hands resting in the West, her feet resting in the East. Sometimes she has a water pot on her head, representing the womb. The water pot likely also references the waters of life: when the Nile flooded each year, it would irrigate the crops, bringing new life and fertility to the land. Nut is also sometimes shown as a cow suckling her many children, or as a sycamore tree, a symbol that is shared by many ancient goddesses.

One unique feature of Nut is that in most ancient cultures, the Earth is gendered female while the sky is gendered male. Here, the opposite is true. The sky is often seen as a sort of immovable force, somewhat distant from Earth and its inhabitants. But here she is, alive, actively giving birth to the Sun, stars, and cosmos, looking after her children both intimately and cosmically. Wherever we may be on Earth, whatever our world may look like, the cosmos is out there, blanketing our world in beauty, ever present, and ready to receive us when it's time to go.

When we think of Mother, we tend to think of birth, life, and creativity. While those are indeed important aspects of the Mother Goddess, it's important also to remember that she holds death as well. Nut was worshiped most often at the end of life. She can help us hold our own mortality, to hold our loved ones after they pass away. Ancient goddesses like Nut remind us that birth and death are much closer than we like to think.

As the eternal, immovable sky, Nut holds us with the kind of endless patience and compassion that's impossible for our human mothers—even the best ones. Looking up at the night sky, especially when we can see the Moon and all the stars, can remind us of how little we are, of how much bigger the universe is than we can even begin to fathom. Nut's motherhood is like that—not human, not limited, not tainted by the stresses of everyday life. It just is, forever, from the beginning to the end and back again. Nut has none of the limitations of our human mothers or ourselves in the role of mother. Her patience is wider than the Earth itself. Whatever is going on for us, no matter how much pain we are in and even to the moment of death, she is with us, on our side, not going anywhere.

Goddess energy is not about judging, punishing, or granting wishes. Rather, she witnesses. She does not control our lives for us, but can be with us when we are suffering or feeling lost. Whether we talk to her or not, she's there. Whether we make good or bad choices, she's there. Whether we suffer or experience joy, she's with us. If we ever forget that, all we need to do is look up

MEDITATION WITH NUT:

Resting in sky

Set your circle and acknowledge the land you are on. Consider Nut's land, ancient Egypt, and your relationship with that part of the world and its wisdom. Do this meditation at night, whether sitting in the dark with a candle lit, outside observing the stars, or as you are falling asleep for the night.

When you're ready, begin to focus on your breath. Notice, specifically, the moment between your exhale and the next inhale. There is a tiny pause there at the bottom of the breath, a nothing, a darkness, a moment before. Notice what it feels like when breath floods in again, bringing life, energy, and possibility. You may let the breath out gently if you want to explore that, or simply observe the natural pause as it is.

Begin to imagine the night sky within that pause. It is expansive, endless, beautiful, and dark. But it is also bright, filled with stars, planets, galaxies far beyond your comprehension. It's up there right now, embracing you and the earth you rest on.

Feel the way this wide expanse holds you completely, no matter what's going on in your life, no matter what mistakes you've made. Nut is the stardust you came from and the stardust to which you will one day return. There is nothing to fear in this darkness, in this pause.

Let Nut hold you. Talk to her if you like. She will listen to anything you have to say. Then listen to her responses, taking in her vast wisdom.

When this process feels complete for you, thank the land, the circle, your breath, and the depthless, endless night sky, the Mother Goddess Nut.

MARY: THE DIVINE VIRGIN

Once upon a time, there was a very rich couple named Anna and Joachim. They shared their wealth with the people and the temple, and wanted for nothing but a child. They waited and wished and prayed, but no child came to them.

At last, Joachim went to the wilderness to fast and pray for 40 days and 40 nights. Left on her own, Anna wandered in her garden. One day, she came upon a laurel tree with a bird's nest in its branches, filled with perfect eggs. Anna sat down and cried:

> "Woe is me! What am I like? I'm not like the birds of heaven, because even the birds of heaven are fruitful before you, Lord.
>
> "Woe is me! What am I like? I'm not like the animals, because even the animals are fruitful before you, Lord.
>
> "Woe is me! What am I like? I'm not like the wild beasts of the Earth, because even the wild beasts of the Earth are fruitful before you, Lord."[3]

Spirit heard Anna and Joachim's prayers and was moved. An angel appeared to Anna, telling her that she would bear a child who would become known throughout the world, famous for centuries. Anna felt the sudden fluttering of life in her womb. She fell to her knees in gratitude and hope as her husband returned from the wilderness to hear the good news. Anna and Joachim promised the angel that their child would be in the service of God forever.

Sure enough, a beautiful baby girl was born, and she was named Mary, Star of the Sea, the one who appears like a miracle from the chaos of the ocean. Right away, Mary knew who she was. She knew the world needed her, and she was ready to do whatever it took to be there for her people.

When Anna brought her to the temple, Mary danced on the steps. She stayed with the temple priestesses, spinning silk and weaving cloth, washing the bloodstained linens of the priests who made sacrifices to their God. Every night, the angel would greet her, feeding her from his hand, telling her truths and prophesies. Mary understood it all, even if it sometimes brought tears to her eyes.

But when Mary reached the age of twelve, the temple priest Zechariah began to worry that she would start her monthly blood and want a husband. Mary wanted no such thing, but to continue to spend her life in contemplation and prayer with women and angels. Zechariah loved Mary and felt there was something special in her, and he didn't know what to do. He prayed, and the angel appeared, telling him to ask all the widowers of the town to bring a staff and place it on the temple altar. God would then send a sign.

They did so, and the widowers' staffs were placed on the darkened altar for three nights. On the third night, one, a sycamore fig, began to flower. It belonged to the carpenter Joseph, whose staff had been passed down for generations through his family from the time of King David. When the widowers returned, Joseph was surprised to find his old staff now heavy with clusters of tiny green and white flowers. Zechariah blessed him as the betrothed of the temple's beloved priestess Mary.

Joseph agreed to protect the young girl and keep her safe, but he did not want to perform the role of a husband. He already had children and he was an old man compared to this young innocent woman, barely out of childhood. Mary continued to spin and weave the silk for the temple veils, happily serving God in Joseph's house rather than the temple. He was gentle and kind and didn't ask Mary for anything.

One day, when Joseph was away for work, Mary's angel came to her and let her know the time had come for her to bear her child. He was to be a hero, a very special child who was destined to change the world. Mary had known this was coming from all the angel had told her at the temple. But she was afraid, too, because she knew she did not live in a world that would easily accept this divine conception.

When Joseph returned, he found his soon-to-be wife pregnant with child. He was shocked and afraid, ashamed that he had not protected the girl well enough while he was away. He lay restless in his bed at night, and resolved to end the engagement quietly, to protect her and himself from shame and ridicule. But an angel cast him into sleep and appeared in a dream, reassuring him that all was well and he could trust this Virgin Mary. Joseph believed in the angel's message and held to his faith that God would protect them both.

In time, the priest Zechariah came to check on his favorite priestess. He saw her swollen belly and gasped. He insisted that Joseph and Mary face the trial of the bitter water at the temple. Mary knew this trial was intended to kill anyone who was not telling the truth, but she was not afraid. Joseph and Mary held to their faith and drank the bitter water, which took them into a wilderness where visions of angels, thieves, the end of one world and the beginning of another, disturbed and reassured them. When they returned from their journeys unharmed, the priest blessed them and let them go.

But the couple had another trial to face. The Roman emperor Caesar Augustus had sent out a decree requiring that everyone register in their homeland. Joseph had to leave Galilee for Bethlehem, where his family was from, and register Mary as his wife. This would be a journey of several days, and Mary was getting close to the time of her labor. As the two rode along on Joseph's tired old donkeys, Joseph watched Mary's face shifting strangely from soft smiles to sudden tears. He asked her what was wrong.

"I see great joy, dear Joseph, but I also see pain and suffering. I know the future that awaits us is a difficult one, but a beautiful one, too."

As the couple got closer to Bethlehem, the light grew short; it was the winter solstice. Mary could feel the child in her stirring, ready to come out. She told Joseph she needed to stop. Joseph tried to find a place for Mary to lie down, but all the inns were full. Mary was with her angel, however, who showed her the perfect place: a nearby cave with soft hay and a few sleeping animals making it warm and friendly for her and her coming child.

Mary settled there and Joseph ran to try to find a midwife, despite Mary's reassurances that she didn't need one. As he ran, the Moon covered the Sun, the world darkened, and time stood still. The birds stopped their movement mid-flight. The grasses were silent in the wind. A brilliant star appeared in the dark sky, shining directly overhead. Joseph marveled, and all of a sudden a midwife was before him. He explained the situation and brought her to the cave to help Mary, but when they got there, it was all aglow, a strange cloud covering Mary. Then, with a flash of light, the cloud was gone, and Mary was sitting there peacefully, a perfect healthy baby boy at her breast.

Mary felt joy and sorrow settle on her heart, knowing she held her beautiful son on the eve of the birth of the annual Sun. She knew her son would have to die and be reborn each year just like the Sun, and she would share sorrow and rejoice with him equally, just as all the Mothers of God before her had done since the beginning of time.

MARY: RETURN OF THE GODDESS

The Virgin Mary, Mother of God, the Queen of Heaven, is beloved by Christians (and many non-Christians) all over the world. She is a symbol of all that is feminine, divine, and loving, a gentle and compassionate counterpart to the judging and sometimes punishing Christian God.

Mary is only spoken about briefly in the canonical books of the New Testament. In those, her virginity is a question of some debate. The "virgin" birth is a common motif in Greek mythology, which was certainly present at this time, where heroes were often semi-divine, born of a god and a human woman. Several women in the Old and New Testament, including Mary's cousin Elizabeth, who bore John the Baptist, were given children by God after a period of infertility.

One of the words that is used to describe Mary is *parthenos*, a Greek word that means "maiden" or "young girl." It was also an alternate name for Athena Parthenos, whose temple, the Parthenon, still stands in Athens (and served as a church dedicated to Mary in the sixth century CE). Hera, Artemis, and Hestia were also known as virgin goddesses along with Isis, Astarte, and Ishtar, despite the fact that many of these goddesses had established consorts. At the time, the word that's been translated as "virgin" likely did not refer to sexual intercourse at all, and meant something more like "one unto herself." A virgin was a woman who was powerful in and of herself, without the influence of a man.

From this word we also get *parthenogenesis*, which means asexual reproduction. Some animals are capable of this feat, but only the Goddess has been able to create something from nothing, and she's done that easily since the beginning of time. It is understood that Mary did not "know a man" before the angel told her it was her time to bear a child, but her virginity symbolizes much more than that.

Mary is only the latest woman in a long line of "virgins" who gave birth to gods.

The official stance of the Catholic Church is that Mary is *not* a goddess. But she is the Mother of God and she is special. While God is owed *latria*, or supreme worship, and the saints may receive *dulia*, respect and adoration, Mary gets her own category of devotion, called *hyperdulia*. She may not be called Goddess, but she certainly holds that place, especially for the people whose older goddesses were forcibly taken away.

In its pursuit of global evangelism, the Church found that many people would not convert to Christianity unless they could maintain their old traditions (even on pain of death). So it found ways to fold the old ways into the new ones. Yule, the ancient pagan winter solstice festival celebrating the birth of the Sun, became Christmas, a winter solstice festival celebrating the birth of the Son. Lughnasadh, a harvest festival held on August first, became Loaf Mass Day. Imbolc, the ancient feast day of the Celtic goddess Brigid, held on February first, became the feast day of the Catholic St. Brigid of Kildare, also held on February first. It was forbidden to worship the old goddesses, but the people found their essence anew in Mary, Mother of God. As Anne Baring and Jules Cashford point out in their book *The Myth of the Goddess: Evolution of an Image*, images of Mary are creative, prolific, and varied while, "in art, for the most part, Jesus is either a newly born infant or dead!"

Much of the lore about Mary is not found in the canonical New Testament. Many of the stories and images we associate with Mary come from apocryphal texts that were related to biblical content but not included in the official Bible. The story above is inspired by the poetic and miracle-filled Gospel of James, which sees Mary as special from the beginning, something of a virgin birth herself.

The Gospel of James is imbued with magic, with angels feeding Mary from their hands, ancient staffs blooming with miraculous flowers, and a birth, devoid of the pain and sin attributed to Eve, blessed by a special star. Mary is sometimes called Morning Star or *Stella Maris*,

Star of the Sea. Isis, Ishtar, Inanna, and Aphrodite (Venus, for the Romans), are all associated with the morning star. In the centuries of art dedicated to the Virgin Mary, she is often shown standing on a crescent moon, wearing a crown of twelve stars, an image pulled from the Book of Revelations. She shares her official color, blue, with Inanna, which represents purity and the power of the sky and the sea. Blue was once more precious than gold, as it could only be created from crushing Inanna's sacred stone, lapis lazuli.

Mary is also *Mater Dolorosa*, Our Lady of Sorrows, a lamenting goddess whose sacred tears of sorrow and compassion have the power to heal. Even today, people report the miracle of seeing real tears falling from statues of the Mother of God.

According to legend, Isis sits by the Nile river every year to cry for the loss of her husband, Osiris, who was sacrificed to the Underworld. Her tears flow so abundantly they cause the Inundation, the annual flooding of the Nile. Inanna laments her husband Dumuzi, god of shepherds, who was sacrificed to the Underworld to account for her sins, and her bitter mourning brings on winter. Demeter does the same when her daughter is sacrificed to the Underworld for six months of the year, bringing on the desperate cold of Demeter's grief. Even the Chinese Buddhist goddess Quan Yin cries tears for the suffering and pain of humanity. Mary may not be an official goddess, but there is no question she is a part of that lineage.

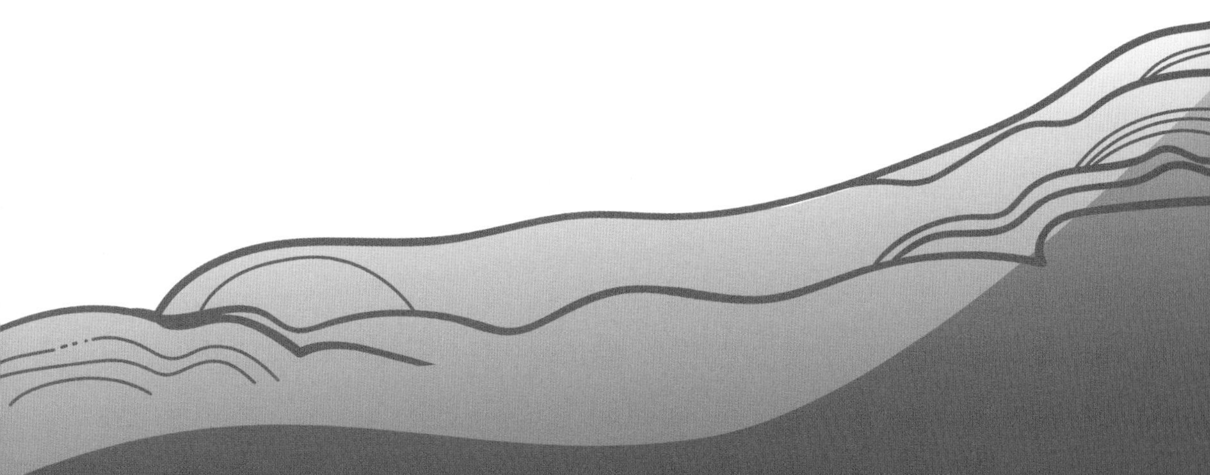

MARY, GODDESS OF COMPASSION

Like Nut, Mary represents the ideal mother, the one with the endless patience and compassion that is only possible for a goddess. Those of us who were raised Christian may have a complex relationship with the Virgin Mary, especially if we were expected to emulate her. Virginity as a literal concept has been upheld for women and girls in ways that can be very damaging for our sexual safety and self-esteem. Mary is the perfect Mother, one who will sacrifice anything for her family and never lose her patience. The sacrificing mother who puts her needs last and has no boundaries with her family is a role many of us have been roped into, only to find that this strategy tends to lead to resentful moms whose patience (and, often, health) is running thin. It may be best not to take all our mothering (or fertility) advice from the Virgin Mary.

But if we can understand her as a goddess, as a mythic archetype rather than a real human being, we can let go of the pressure to be anything like her and instead let her hold us in all our struggles and confusion, even in our imperfect mothering and with our imperfect mothers. Flawed human beings have always needed someone like her, someone much bigger than us and our human foibles, to hold us in our pain, to understand us at our worst and love us anyway. She can hold us, witness us, cry with us, love us with expansive, divine, endless passion. She can be the Mother we need when we need her.

MEDITATION WITH MARY:

The ideal mother

You may like to prepare for this meditation by lighting a candle. Any candle is fine, but a blue candle or even an artistic one with the Virgin Mary depicted on it is perfect. Set your circle and acknowledge the land you are on and your relationship with this land. You may want to consider Mary's land, too, which started in the Middle East and has expanded to most of the world. If your relationship with Mary is present in your family already, you may want to take a moment to contemplate how that has worked, or not worked, for you and your ancestors.

When you're ready, imagine yourself on a beautiful beach at the edge of a great blue sea.

Pray: offer the sea the longings of your heart, the true need for compassion, witnessing, and care in your pain. Gaze into the ocean until you see an image of the Virgin Mary, Star of the Sea, emerge from the waves. She has a crown of stars, raised by the crescent moon, tears flowing down her face.

She approaches you and meets you on the beach. She is just the Mother you need right now. She has the right words and gestures. Tell her anything you want to tell her. Let her hold you, talk to you, listen, and witness. Share your pain with her. If tears come, remember that they, too, are holy water. Listen to any wisdom Mary has to share with you. Spend as much time with this ideal Mother as you need. When this feels complete, thank Mary for listening, for being your witness. Watch her retreating to the wide blue sea, knowing that she's there for you anytime you need her. All you need to do is ask.

Offer your thanks to the sea, the sky, the stars, the land you are on, your circle of protection, your tears, and your own heart.

CRONE

The Crone archetype is the wise woman, old as dirt, wrinkled and grey with the many years she's lived and many things she's seen. Sometimes she is considered ugly or repulsive, but that's part of her charm: she wants to see if you're wise enough to see the magic past the illusion.

The Crone lives in the waning moon and the new moon, the late fall and winter, seasons of aging, death, and nothingness. She is the ending that brings back the beginning, the Crone that midwifes the Maiden, the death that cycles back to life. Don't make the mistake of turning away from her wisdom, scary though it may seem, as it's always wisdom you need.

THE BABA YAGA AND VASILISA THE BEAUTIFUL

Once upon a time, there was a kind, loving couple who had plenty and gave plenty. They wanted for nothing but a child. They prayed and prayed, to God, to the Sky, and to the Forest, asking for the blessing that would ease the pain in their hearts.

The Baba Yaga heard their prayers when she listened to the wind in the morning. She heard their longing whisper through the trees all afternoon, tapping at the soft dirt at night. They never came and asked her directly (as the Baba Yaga was not interested in being found), but they'd leave offerings from time to time. A lock of hair. An embroidered cloth, adorned with symbols of hope. A cup of ale and a handful of white yarrow.

One night the Yaga felt the woman dreaming. She tossed and turned in her sorrow and desperation, promising to offer the child to the Forest if only her wish was granted. At this, the Yaga knew it was time. Soon enough, the woman became pregnant with a little girl who would be named Vasilisa. The child grew to be beautiful and kind, and her mother taught her how to tell the truth, to understand wildness, and how to respect the spirits of the Forest. In time, the girl's mother fell ill, and came to know that she would die. In a dream, the Baba Yaga told her to create a little doll, a *motanka*, to leave to her daughter after her death. In her last days, the mother did nothing but sew, embroidering magical patterns onto the doll's clothing. "Keep this doll by your side always, Vasilisa," she told her. "Feed it from time to time, give it water to drink, and speak of it to no one. If you ever need anything, ask and the doll will help you."

Vasilisa did as she was told, and the doll was there to comfort the girl after her mother breathed her last breath. Years passed, and Vasilisa's father remarried. This new woman was very beautiful, the picture of kindness when her father was around, but cruel and hateful when he was not, which was often. Vasilisa had hoped her new stepsisters would be friends and playmates, but they were often vicious, making her clean out the wood stove and the fireplace and then making fun of the cinders in her hair. Vasilisa only did what she was told, never complaining, never speaking a harsh word, and her magical *motanka* secretly helped her with the chores while she slept.

Through all this, the Yaga watched and waited.

As time went on, Vasilisa maintained her beauty and kindness, and many suitors asked to marry her. Her stepmother refused them all, wanting her own daughters to be married first. Vasilisa's stepsisters' cruelty smelled through their skin, however, and no suitors came for them. When word came that the Tsar himself was looking for a bride amongst the people, Stepmother panicked—she could not have Vasilisa overshadow her daughters again. The Baba Yaga felt her opportunity and sent Stepmother a dream.

The next morning, Stepmother doused all the fires in the house. A chill fell as she called on Vasilisa. "Girl, we need fire. Go to the Baba Yaga's house in the woods and bring us back a coal so we can heat the house again. We are depending on you, dear girl." Stepmother's teeth dripped with sweetness as she smiled. Vasilisa had heard the rumors that the Baba Yaga liked to eat children, and had a feeling her stepmother hoped this was true. But she also remembered her mother's stories about the magic of the Forest, and her curiosity was stronger than her fear. She agreed without argument. The Baba Yaga felt the ground quiver when the girl began the journey. She could feel the doll wanting to come home to her. She knew it wouldn't be long now before she met the sweet girl. Too sweet, she thought. Might need some seasoning.

Days passed, and the Yaga felt the girl and her doll coming closer. At last, they arrived at the fence, exhausted and dirty. Vasilisa stood in awe, taking in the fence, which was made of human bones, adorned with skulls, and the strange little hut, as tall as the treetops, held up by giant chicken legs. Indeed, it was scratching at the dirt as if looking for worms. The Yaga sucked at her pipe in amusement, watching as Vasilisa kept trying to come round to the front of the hut, but no matter which way she walked, she could only see its back. The *motanka* giggled a little as well, letting Vasilisa struggle, until she reminded her of the magic words her mother had taught her.

"Hut, hut, turn your back to the Forest and your front toward me!"

Sure enough, the hut turned around, showing its odd face to her, then settled in the dirt, opening its door-mouth to let her in. Vasilisa stood at the threshold and stared into the darkness. There sat the Baba Yaga, smoking her pipe, staring at the girl, appraising her as if she was a cut of meat. She was a deeply ugly old woman with loose, wild hair and a hooked nose, one leg appearing to be nothing but a single bone.

"Sweet, sweet," the Yaga murmured. "Too sweet. You hold everyone's bitter so you can be sweet, eh, little girl?" The Yaga's bushy eyebrows lifted, surveying her child.

Vasilisa gathered her courage. "Grandmother..." she started. "My name is Vasilisa. My family's fire has gone out. I am here to ask for an ember from your fire to bring back to them."

Baba Yaga laughed, a delighted, hearty laugh. "Yes, well. Let's get to the seasoning then, shall we?"

Vasilisa only looked at her, waiting for a command, a gift, or to be shoved in the oven, she wasn't sure which.

"Well, girl, nothing comes for free. I will give you the fire if you can work for it. If you cannot," the Yaga's eyes blackened like char, "You shall feed my hungry oven." The girl paled, glancing at the giant wood stove in the corner of the hut.

"First, you will separate the good corn from the rotten." Out of nowhere, a giant pile of corn appeared. "If it is not done by the time I return, my oven will have its meal!" The Yaga cackled and jumped into a giant mortar that lifted into the air and flew away.

Vasilisa struggled to tell the difference between the good corn and the mildewed corn. She took the little doll out of her pocket and it sprang to life, ready to help her. As the two worked, the corn's hallucinogenic magic took over, sending Vasilisa into a strange sleep full of dreams of death and the otherworld. The seasoning had begun.

When the Baba Yaga returned, the task was complete. She pretended to be surprised. "Well then, child, a second task for you. Separate the poppy seeds from the dirt in the yard. If this task is not done when I return, my oven and I will eat you for dinner!" Again, she jumped into her mortar and flew away.

The girl and her *motanka* worked all night separating the tiny poppy seeds from the grains of dirt. As they worked, the poppyseed nectar stained Vasilisa's hands, entering her nose and skin, bringing her visions of the world between worlds, justice and death. Vasilisa understood all, but didn't remember a thing when she came to, finding a perfect pile of clean poppy seeds next to a plain pile of dirt.

The Yaga returned, again pretending to be surprised, hiding her pleasure that the girl was doing so well. She could see some lines of understanding in Vasilisa's once-perfect face now, the touch of age and death around her eyes making her all the more beautiful.

"You've done well, girl. Let us eat." The Yaga brought fresh bread, honey, and salt to the table. Vasilisa stared at her, eyes wide.

"It's not poisoned, if that's what you're worried about." Vasilisa couldn't help her hunger and tucked in, gratefully chewing the warm, soft bread. "You'd need a little more flesh on your bones to be a good meal for my oven, anyway." The Yaga laughed, and the slightest smile flitted across Vasilisa's pretty face. The Yaga took a puff of her pipe, noticing that the girl would pinch a crumb every now and then and slip it into her pocket, feeding her doll. She had listened well to her mother.

"Tell me, child. It is not easy to find me and my little hut. How did you come to be this way?"

The girl paused. "By the blessing of my mother," she said.

The Yaga frowned. Her eyes darkened once again. "This is not a place of blessings. You came here of your own courage and ability. You must learn to take your own credit, idiot girl." The Yaga stood, turning her rancor towards the girl, rising to her full fearsomeness, feeling the girl cower.

"It is time for your third and final task. I will give you the fire. Bring it through the Forest and return it to your family. If you survive, so be it. If you do not, my oven will get its meal after all." She reached deep into the wood stove, and pulled out a human skull, the embers inside making its eyes dance. She handed the fiery skull to the girl.

Vasilisa took it, fearful, but some part of her remembered the lessons from her strange visions, and she knew the skull would not burn her. "Thank you, Grandmother," she said, bowing lightly. She and her doll fled back into the dark Forest.

Baba Yaga watched from the treetops as Vasilisa returned to her stepmother, who was cold and thin, having been unable to light so much as a candle while Vasilisa was gone. The girl bowed gently and offered the embers but, as the Yaga expected, Stepmother cast the skull down in fear and disgust. Sure enough, its bones broke and the fire spread throughout the house as if it was hungry, devouring everything in its path. Vasilisa ran to safety and found herself outside, not a cinder on her. And just like that, the evil stepmother and her too-bitter girls burnt to ashes, never to be seen again.

THE BABA YAGA: MISTRESS OF THE FOREST

Vasilisa the Beautiful (or The Wise or The Brave) is just one of the many Slavic folktales that feature the Baba Yaga. The Yaga is an ambiguous figure in tales like these, sometimes helping the hero or heroine, sometimes cooking them in her magical oven. She is always grotesquely ugly and very old. She flies around in a mortar with no pestle, but often carries a broom. Her magical hut wanders around on giant chicken legs, never committing to one location. To this day, the Baba Yaga is something of a boogeyman, a story told to children to scare them into behaving.

The Baba Yaga first appeared in writings about Slavic folktales in the eighteenth century, but, like many of the goddesses we've met in this book, she likely had a long oral history before anything was committed to writing. She still shows up in pop culture today, though not always by that name. She is likely the witch with the candy house in the story of Hansel and Gretel. You might recognize some of the themes of Cinderella in the story above—many versions of this story end with Vasilisa marrying the Tsar. She has appeared in movies and TV shows as the archetype of the Witch of the Forest, a magical being who might help you or might kill you, depending on whether or not she deems you worthy.

Many of the Baba Yaga tales are, essentially, horror stories. As a genre, horror has always been a way to contain and process social anxieties. A story can take an abstract concept like death, plague, or otherness and make it concrete, as monsters or aliens. We may feel some sort of catharsis in seeing our anxiety made manifest and then defeated. The Baba Yaga may represent the metaphorical monster that is women's power, especially women who are unmarried, reject social expectations, or do not want children.

During the centuries-long witch hunts that happened all over the world, the people most frequently targeted as witches by Christian authorities were women who had any sort of power that might undermine that of the Church at the time, especially in its connection with patriarchy and capitalism. This meant herbalists, folk healers, and midwives, especially if they had any knowledge of abortion or contraception. Sometimes it was women who refused a man's sexual advances or widows who were uninterested in being remarried. The "witches" became evil inversions of these regular people: poison makers, baby-eaters, husband-killers, ugly old women uninterested in men, sexual slaves of the Devil, and so on.

The motif of cooking and eating children recurs consistently in the Baba Yaga tales. This could have provided something of a social scapegoat during the long eras of plague and starvation when babies and children died frequently and often mysteriously. The idea that a witch was coming to take these children away meant that someone could be blamed for this real-life horror, making it easier to understand and process. On the other hand, some see the Baba Yaga as a goddess of the Underworld, much like Persephone, who gently shepherded these lost babies into their afterlife. The Yaga's oven could also be a symbol for the womb, the symbolic experience of "baking" in the transformative heat before birth/rebirth. The Baba Yaga could also be Old Woman Winter, who "eats" the Maiden Spring and gives birth to her again at the winter solstice.

The Baba Yaga was likely a sort of forest deity—The Mistress of the Forest—before she got the Christian witch-washing. Like the Celtic Morrígan sisters, the Baba Yaga is a protector of the wild, and can be as benevolent or violent as nature itself. She also lives in liminal places, like the fae, slipping in and out of human reality, only being found when she wants to be. The Baba Yaga holds the ambiguity of many of our ancient goddess figures: she is neither good nor bad, but presides over death and rebirth, hope and loss, dark and light.

THE BABA YAGA: THE DARK MOTHER

The Baba Yaga teaches us about aging, death, and connection with the underworld. She is a teacher of dark, true things. Life is not all rainbows and light. Death, horror, sickness, loss, grief, rage, anger, and injustice are parts of the world—the seasonings Vasilisa the Innocent needs. In order to become whole, a fully developed person, Vasilisa the Maiden must be consumed by the Crone so that she can be processed, digested, refined by the process of separating the good corn from the mildewed, the poppy seeds from the dirt.

Vasilisa learns to manage the Baba Yaga not by thinking logically, but by listening to the magical doll in her pocket, a symbol for her intuition. The tasks of the mildewed corn and poppy seeds may reference ancient practices of fermenting corn and squeezing oil from poppy seeds to create altered states of consciousness, ritualized experiences where we could escape the strictures of the conscious mind and see the truth beyond the visible.

At the end of the story, the Baba Yaga gifts Vasilisa with a skull filled with fiery light. Whether we like it or not, we meet this skull light—the light of death—from time to time in our lives. We are forced to hold this terrifying thing, the realities of darkness, death, pain, and regret, and must learn to hold it gently, lovingly, to remember that it is a gift. The Crone may seem to be as far from the Maiden as anything can get, but the opposite is true: they are two ends of a line, meeting at the new moon, the winter solstice, the door between death and life, creating a circle.

MEDITATION WITH BABA YAGA:

The gift of death light

This meditation is best when facing the death light: if someone you love has died or you are facing your own mortality. You could also do this on a new or waning moon, on the darkest days of winter, or on October 31st, a day when the veils between the worlds thin. This meditation will allow some time to be with darker emotions. If you're not in the right place to receive the Yaga's medicine today, come back when you're feeling more up to the task.

If you have a skull, a picture of a skull, a memorial item, or some other visual symbol of death, please have it ready. You can also use your imagination. Darken the room and light a candle. Settle in, casting your circle and acknowledging the land.

Contemplate this image of death. Let your eyes soften or close as you gaze at your symbol. You can also imagine the Baba Yaga's death light: the skull with fiery eyes staring back at you. Keep breathing. Sit with the concepts of loss, death, dying, and the way the world looks when the death light is present. Rather than turning away, allow the energy of death to be present. Bathe in its medicine. Don't rush too quickly to rebirth and renewal—those energies will come, but it's not yet time for that.

If you are angry, sad, confused, or anything else, simply let that be. Don't turn away from that sacred seasoning. Offer these thoughts and feelings into the womb of the Baba Yaga's oven.

When this feels complete, thank the death light and the Baba Yaga for all they have to teach you. Close your circle and blow out the candle. Be tender with yourself now and make sure you are not trying to numb out the magic of the death light. Let it keep working on you. The light will return, it always does, but not before the darkness is allowed to do its work.

DHUMAVATI: GODDESS OF DESPAIR AND DISAPPOINTMENT

Once upon a time, when the universes were continually being created and destroyed like bubbles in a pot, the gods got in trouble. Shiva, the god of destruction, was so deep in his meditation that he wasn't doing his work destroying the universes so new ones could be created. The balance of everything was off, and Brahma, the Creator, and Vishnu, the Sustainer, needed to wake Shiva from his deep trance. They asked, they requested, they demanded, they cajoled, they even poked him a little, but still Shiva would not stir.

So the gods did what they must always do when they are really in trouble and need some help: they asked for their Mama. The gods got together and prayed, petitioning the Great Goddess, Shakti, to help them. Shakti, hearing their prayer, appeared before them as a beautiful woman with kind eyes and wisdom beyond her apparent years. The gods bowed before their Mother so low that pieces of gold and gemstones fell from their crowns at her feet.

"I will help you," she told them. "But on one condition. You must never forget who I am. If you do, I will return to my immaterial form, and you'll have to fight your battles on your own."

The gods all agreed, sure they'd never forget the great Shakti's power and supremacy. They only existed because of her, after all. How could they possibly forget?

So it was that Shakti took form as a beautiful woman named Sati, and went to meet Shiva on his mountaintop. As she stood before him, he felt something he had never felt before—the stirrings of desire. He opened his eyes and saw a woman with glowing skin, beautiful curves, and the lines of intelligence in her face. He suddenly knew he wanted her as a part of his life. She took his hand, and her gentle warmth overcame him. The two embraced and made love for a few millennia, with Sati initiating Shiva into the pleasures of the flesh, the joy of breath, the meaning of a moment. When they at last took rest from their love games, Sati gently showed Shiva the results of his absence in the universes. It was time to allow things to come to an end so that Brahma and Vishnu could get back to their work of creating and sustaining. Shiva immediately understood and got back to work, bringing the universes back into balance.

Time passed in peace and prosperity. One day, Daksha, the *deva* who had been assigned to play the role of Sati's father, wanted to have a celebration. He had grown into great riches and respect within the divine community as a religious leader. He was to have a great fire ceremony, inviting all the who's who of the universes. He did not, however, invite Shiva. He didn't like his blue skin, so often stained with the ashes from the cremation grounds. He didn't approve of his dreadlocks and usually mostly unclothed state. He was uncomfortable with the reminder of death and endings, which were not a welcome part of his growing empire.

Shiva didn't much mind this. He wasn't one for big religious ceremonies, and truly would rather hang out with the dead than go to these pompous parties. But when she heard the news, Sati was furious. Her eyes turned black and her skin turned grey. Fangs appeared in her teeth and she snarled, a flash of blood red in her mouth. Shiva had never seen this side of his Sati and was concerned.

"What does it matter, my love? I do not want to go anyway."

"You do not understand," Sati growled. "None of you understand. They have broken the promise. You have all forgotten who I am. I am the one who should be honored at the ceremony, but instead I am excluded, my chosen husband ignored. They have forgotten why they needed me to be Sati in the first place, because they needed you!" Sati stormed off, lightning in her footsteps, and Shiva chased after her, trying to calm her down, to tell her to let it go. But she would not.

Sati appeared at the party with embers smoldering in her eyes. Her father stood next to the giant fire, holding court over the many devas in their finery. He shivered as she approached him. "Hello daughter," Daksha smiled uncomfortably.

"You mean *Mother*," Sati hissed. She stared him down, her eyes flickering with depthless black flames. Without another word, Sati stepped into the ceremonial fire, becoming one with the flames, returning to her original form as the immaterial Shakti, the energy of everything, the Great Goddess.

As the gathered crowd looked on in shock, Shiva fell to his knees, wailing horribly, his great love gone forever. He tore at his hair, and from a dreadlock that fell to the ground, a warrior rose from the dirt, a giant sword in his hand. With one great slice, the warrior cut off Daksha's head. Overwhelmed by his grief, Shiva returned to the mountains, finding an even higher, even more remote cave to meditate in. He would not return to his work again for a very, very long time.

From the smoke of the fire, a new image appeared. An ugly old woman, her face wrinkled, her hollow cheeks hungry, her breasts dry. She surveyed the carnage quietly, her eyes filled with grief. A giant crow settled at her side, and a serpent slid around her neck. She held a broom, but had no threshold to sweep. She had a winnowing basket, but no wheat to process. A skull appeared at her side, upturned and empty. Behind her was a carriage, but it no horse to draw it. Dhumavati, the goddess of disappointment and despair, had been born.

DHUMAVATI THE WIDOW

Dhumavati is a part of the Hindu Shakta Tantra tradition of India, where the Goddess is supreme in her many forms. Tantra took hold around the sixth century CE as an offshoot of Hinduism, which may be the oldest sustaining religion in the world, dating back to about 3000 BCE. The story above is a tantric perspective on another, older story, that places the god Shiva as the hero. In that version, Sati is a devoted wife who threw herself onto the fire when her husband was insulted by not being invited to the fire ceremony. This became the model for a disturbing practice where widows in some communities in India would end their lives on their husband's funeral pyres. This practice was called *sati*.

Dhumavati is a widow, which is possibly the most inauspicious position one could have in Indian society. Even today, in some cases, widows are abandoned by their families and forced to live alone or in special ashrams. They are required to wear white, the color of mourning, and shave their heads. Some are blamed for their husband's death. They are outcast, no longer worth anything without a man to validate their existence. The practice of *sati* was outlawed by the British colonists with the aid of Hindu reformers in the 1800s, but it has been seen here and there into more modern times. As awful as it was, some women may have chosen it willingly, preferring death in the fire to life as a widow.

The Tantrikas, like Dhumavati and the widows, lived on the edge of society. Tantrikas would go to the places that mainstream Hindus generally avoided, like the cremation grounds. Sometimes their practices included secret rituals involving sex and animal sacrifice. They were fascinated by the darker side of life, and explored the deepest truth of Goddess worship: that Goddess, or Shakti, is truly *everything*—the dirt, the gold, the garbage, the luck of good wealth, and the desperate experience of widowhood.

In one of Dhumavati's origin stories, Shiva and Sati are spending time together when Sati asks Shiva for something to eat (which could be a metaphor for sexual desire). He refuses, and she becomes angry, deciding to eat him instead, engulfing him in a single bite. She eventually sets him free, and he curses her to become a widow, turning her into Dhumavati.

One way of reading this story is that Sati was reminding Shiva that he only exists by her grace, that she is one unto herself—the original definition of "virgin." Shakti is the chaos that existed before the Big Bang. Without the masculine, she is pure, unformed energy. But when the masculine joins her, it can give her shape and consciousness, create form out of chaos. He cannot exist without her, but she has always been, with or without him. If she's hungry, she will eat.

As a white woman raised on patriarchal Christianity where God was an all-powerful Father "up there," I craved a spirituality that included me, my body, and my experience more fully. I found Tantra through yoga and my many (usually white) yoga teachers who told fascinating stories about goddesses who often had more power than the gods. I read the British colonist and lover of Tantra, Arthur Avalon, also known as Sir John Woodroffe, who translated several tantric texts into English in the early 1900s; and Douglas Brooks, a present-day university professor who spent decades in India trying to understand Tantra. Even though I knew there were complexities here I couldn't fully grasp from my white, northerner perspective, I fell in love with Tantra and its goddesses, the ugly ones as well as the beautiful. These goddesses taught me about the radical practice of non-rejection, of seeing power even in powerlessness. The fact that Dhumavati exists means there is value to be found in loss, despair, grief, and disappointment—and we can all relate to those, no matter where we grew up or what we believe.

Dhumavati has a particular resonance with the Baba Yaga, the Witch of the Woods. Both are particularly ugly old crones who can be found at the edges of society. Both have that witchiest of accessories, a broom, and both carry a special skull. They are feared, but also have great powers to help and protect those that are willing to work with them. It's not known for sure if the Baba Yaga and Dhumavati are related, but they could be—we do know that Sanskrit, India's ancient language, has the same Indo-Aryan root as the Slavic languages. As sentinels of the worst positions in society according to patriarchal rules, Dhumavati and the Baba Yaga are freed of the burden of the male gaze—which means they get to make their own rules.

DHUMAVATI THE WITNESS

Dhumavati is worshiped by some and avoided by others. She is seen as inauspicious, not exactly an energy you'd want to invite into your life. But when you're already there at the edge of the cremation grounds, lost, alone, frustrated, and in despair, Dhumavati understands. She can meet you in that place. She can feel the depth of the disappointment with you and not turn away. She is a reminder that there is divine magic—Shakti—in everything, no matter how bad things have gotten.

Dhumavati is old and ugly, skinny and sick-looking. She's got an empty carriage and no horse, the epitome of a woman going nowhere. In one of her four hands, she carries a winnowing basket which separates the wheat from the chaff. Like Baba Yaga's task of separating the poppy seeds from the dirt, it is these difficult experiences at the edge of what we know where we truly learn discernment. In our darkest times, we discover who our friends are. We learn something about the nature of the universe, which is powerful, if not always benevolent. We get much better at telling the difference between reality and illusion.

In another hand, Dhumavati holds a broom, a symbol of domesticity for someone who has no home. But the broom can also sweep away negativity, impurities, and illusion. It is sometimes associated with the transformative properties of the hearth fire, and of course it is a witch's preferred vehicle.

A third hand holds a gesture of gift-giving and the fourth a gesture of wisdom. These are indications that Dhumavati may not be as terrifying as she first appears. Her darkness and disappointment come with gifts, and some of her texts even say she will give her worshippers anything they want. She is also sometimes named "tender hearted," the one who offers compassion and care in these difficult times. She is one of the Ten Great Wisdom goddesses, the *Dasa Mahavidyas*, a group of fierce tantric goddesses. These goddesses embody ten aspects of the Great Goddess that range from youth and beauty to fierce warrior, and Dhumavati's ugly, lonely misery.

Sometimes Dhumavati is seen with a skull held upside down like a cup you can drink from. This connects her with Shiva, the god of death, destruction, and endings, who wears a garland of skulls and holds another in his hand (which likely once belonged to Sati's 'father' Daksha). Like the Baba Yaga, Dhumavati offers the death light, the nectar that can be tasted at the edge of life and death.

Dhumavati is especially powerful when we've lost our hope. When we feel carved out, like there's nothing left, Dhumavati asks us to stay present, to feel the depths of what we are feeling, to notice the powerful energy of loss, pain, grief, and isolation. If we can keep feeling these painful things without shutting down, we may be able to find the gems and riches inside them. Even if you've never felt more alone, Dhumavati reminds you that she's an archetype for a reason: however much we push it to the edges of our consciousness, her experience is universal. She is universal. If she's with you now, listen closely for her secrets.

MEDITATION WITH DHUMAVATI:

The smoke from the fire

This meditation is best done when you are already in a state of despair, disappointment, or hopelessness, or if you have some of those feelings to process. If you have the ability to build and douse a fire outside, you can do that, or simply use a candle. You may want to have a journal nearby to write down your thoughts.

Prepare for your meditation by lighting your candle. Set your circle and honor the land you are on, the lands you came from, and Dhumavati's lands.

Gently observe the fire in front of you as you invite your feelings of loss, grief, loneliness, and disappointment to the surface. Notice where you feel them in your body. Notice if they have words. No need to do anything with them right now, just bring them up. Do your best to keep breathing fully, allowing the emotional energy to flow, not shutting it down.

When you're ready, imagine offering this energy into the fire. Feed the fire with your pain and loss. Breathe deeply as you are doing this.

When this feels complete, douse or blow out the fire. Watch the smoke as it rises—this is Dhumavati's domain. See the grey smoke rise and disappear. Imagine Dhumavati witnessing you as you witness her in the form of smoke. Do not take your eyes away. Keep breathing.

When the smoke has disappeared completely, bow to Dhumavati and thank her for witnessing you, for sitting with you in your pain. Journal if you'd like. When the ritual feels complete, honor the land, the Goddess, the fire and smoke, and close the circle.

THE CAILLEACH: THE WINTER QUEEN

Before there was time, in the long eternity of the world, there was nothing but icy ocean and the Cailleach. She was a giant, so big she could walk lightly among the glaciers and skim across the water. Her wrinkled old skin was frostbitten blue and her tusk-like teeth were red as rust. Her single eye could see beyond sight and her garments were decorated with skulls. No one knows whether she made this world or this world made her. As millennia passed, the Cailleach began to feel lonely. She wanted to share her icy world with someone. So it was that she struck her magical hammer down, shaking loose the earth from the bottom of the ocean. From this, she collected giant boulders in her apron and scattered them across this new land, creating the mountains, hills, valleys, glens, and lochs we know today. When she was finished, she lovingly placed her pure white blanket over the hills, coating them with snow.

Then she created others: nine other Cailleachs, just like her, to help shape the new land. They did their work well, but still, the Cailleach was lonely. So she created more and more children of different kinds and types. She created the Moon and the Sun, wolves, eagles, mice, holly trees, and countless other winter creatures who could love her world with her.

But one of these children was different from all the rest. Where her mother's skin was wrinkled, blue, and white, Brigid's was smooth and creamy, with rosy cheeks and a shock of red hair. She was so warm she glowed slightly, her lightest touch able to melt her mother's snow. Sometimes she would lay, belly down, ear to the cold earth, as if she was listening. The Cailleach loved this strange daughter she couldn't understand, and felt the need to keep her safe. So she created a cave for Brigid to stay in and tried her best to make it comfortable according to her daughter's needs. Brigid was happy there, and the two worked and lived together day by day, tending to the simple tasks of everyday life. One evening, mother and daughter talked as they sipped salty ocean water and bit the sharp ends from icicles.

"Mother," said Brigid, "I had a strange dream."

"Tell it, love," her mother said.

"I dreamed of another world, one that is green and warm, where sweet things grow from the earth. There is poetry and music and dancing late into the evening. The people make love, and the love makes new babies that grow up to plant seeds and dance and make more babies."

The Cailleach paused. While she knew there was a time for that world to come, she did not think that time was yet here. She knew that world was not for her, and that its arrival meant her end. "Were you afraid?"

"That's just the thing," Brigid turned her deep green eyes onto her mother's single, ice-blue eye."I loved it. I feel almost as if it's right at my fingertips, that I could simply touch the land and wish that world into existence."

The Cailleach stood. "You shall not. You must stay here where it is safe, with me. Do not think further on this dream." She grumbled to herself, then left her daughter to secure the entrance of the cave, an unusual chill running down her back. But there were things Brigid hadn't told her mother. She hadn't told her of the fire inside her belly that urged her to plunge her hands into the frozen dirt until it softened into clay. To kiss away the ice on the rivers so that they could flow with awesome power. She didn't tell her mother that she'd been pressing her ear to the earth from time to time, listening to the seeds whispering to her, calling her to make them rise and bloom in wild unknown colors like red, purple, and yellow, stretching open in longing to the warm sun. She did not tell her mother that she knew she could no longer stay.

As Brigid dreamed that night, hot in her sleep, she saw a beautiful young man named Aengus, the Ever Young. He sat alone in the Otherworld, playing a golden harp, wishing for true love. Brigid knew right away that she loved him. So Brigid sang songs of lament, so beautiful and pure that they traveled across the veils into the Otherworld where Aengus was asleep and dreaming. He saw Brigid, a woman as beautiful as fire itself, and loved her immediately. He spent his days waiting for sleep so he could dream of her again. He stopped eating and sleeping, becoming sick with his desire for this warm spark in a winter world. He came to know he must find Brigid or die.

It was the time of the Wolf month, however, and Aengus knew the Cailleach would be howling across the sky, riding her winter wolf. But he could not wait for her to come down and rest. So he pulled some magic from the Sun, borrowing three days from August and giving them to February, and went on the quest to find his love. Aengus followed his heart across the treacherous winter lands. He listened with his whole body, attuning to the whistle of the sharp winds, the harsh laughter of the Cailleach, the whirling center of her storms. And at last he heard Brigid singing. Aengus had not escaped the Cailleach's all-seeing eye, however. She watched as he approached the cave. She saw him tune his ears to Brigid's song, the beautiful lilt of her daughter's voice that she loved as well as him, if not more so. She watched her daughter greet her love and run away from the home she had shared with her mother.

This sight broke the Cailleach's heart. She lay down on the earth and expressed her sorrow, for herself, for her daughter, for the end of the world, letting her tears soak the rimy ground. She cried so long and so bitterly she turned into a giant stone, its smooth surface eternally wet with the tears of a mother who had lost her daughter.

Meanwhile, Brigid's heart was afire. The moment she met Aengus, they embraced, and the spark of their kiss was so deep and hot it softened the earth beneath their feet, and a tiny white flower, a snowdrop, appeared from the earth, the first of Brigid's many children. As the lovers ran across the ground, fearing the Cailleach would find them, they left green, grassy footprints, melting the snow, and more flowers burst from the earth as if they'd been waiting all this time to stretch their faces to the sun. The lovers laughed, their joy reverberating across the Earth, creating sheaves of wheat, tall corn stalks, and strawberry flowers that would become sweet red fruit in the shape of their beating hearts. As they dipped their fingers into the rivers and lochs, the ice would melt around their touch and the waters would begin to flow. Even the holly tree, so gnarled and withered, beloved of the Cailleach, brought forth clusters of white flowers.

Forgetting themselves in their dance of love and creation, Brigid and Aengus lay down to rest and make love. They stayed there for a long eternity, holding each other in the heat of passion, creating an abundant spring and an endless summer. But after a while, the wheat began to dry and wither. The holly berries fell to the earth. Tree branches broke and tumbled in the gentle summer breezes. Wildfires started in dry woods, filling the fresh air with smoke. No more flowers rose from the cracked ground. Brigid began to turn away from Aengus, feeling a strange cold grow over her. She missed her mother. When she told Aengus, he felt for her, but the fear of the great Winter Queen pricked his heart. "Do not go looking for her, my love. We could lose this beautiful world we've created," Aengus pleaded.

"But where is the beautiful world she created?" Brigid countered. "And our world is dying anyway. Don't you see it?" Brigid gestured to the landscape, once lush and green, now brown and dry, rusting as red as the Cailleach's teeth. "I must find my mother."

Aengus tried to make her stay, but he was helpless against her will. Brigid listened for the great laughter that would kick up the storms and sharp winds of winter, but heard nothing. She knocked on the earth as her mother had taught her to do, listening for giant footsteps, but the ground was too spent and empty to drum back.

Brigid wept as she searched, fearing that following her heart had killed her mother, but knowing that staying would have killed her self.

At last Brigid returned to the old cave where she had spent so many of her younger days. It was just as she and Aengus had left it, but beside it was a giant stone, cold and slightly moist, as if seeping sorrowful tears. Brigid placed her warm hands on the stone, kissed it gently, and cried her mother's name. Deep inside the stone stirred the grieving heart of the Cailleach. The old woman's bones creaked and cracked as she stretched and rose to see her fiery daughter's green eyes bright with tears. She exhaled, her breath a puff of white in the cold air around her. She embraced her daughter, and the two held each other with ancient love and understanding.

"I am so sorry, mother. I should never have left the cave."

"You're wrong, my girl," said the Cailleach in her characteristically harsh and loving tone. "The world you created was beautiful. But it cannot sustain itself without me, as I cannot sustain myself without you. The seeds need me to hold and contain them now, to let them rest so that you can return when they are ready."

"Return? What do you mean?"

"I will take this world while the Little Sun is in the sky. I will cover this land with snow and let it sleep while you rest with your love. Then, when Beltane comes and the Big Sun is in the sky, I will take my rest. Bring life and growth and babies to my forests and glens. Bring food to the people. Show them dancing and creation and the colors of the flowers, all the things I could never understand. But when Samhain comes and the light withdraws from the evenings, I shall take my turn. I am an old woman, after all. I do need your help, my daughter."

So it was that the Cailleach returned each Samhain, casting her blanket of snow across the land, allowing the seeds to rest. And when she finished her work on Beltane, she would retreat to the Otherworld to rest and slake her thirst at the Holy Well, entrusting Brigid to bless the land with the warmth and joy of spring and summer.

THE CAILLEACH: THE FIRST CRONE

The Cailleach (pronounced many ways, including *KAY-lee-ack*) is one of the most prolific mythic figures of the Celtic world. Many natural formations are named after her, especially in Ireland and Scotland, where legends say she would drop boulders from her apron and let them roll about as they might. She is a giantess, always an old woman. She has one keen eye with the Second Sight. Her skin is white or blue and wrinkled, and she has red teeth. Sometimes she wears a cloak of human skulls. She carries a magical hammer or rod that she bangs on the ground to spread ice and snow. The word *cailleach* in modern Gaelic means "old woman" or "hag."

There are countless stories featuring the Cailleach, many of which contradict each other. The roots of these stories go far back, much further than the written word. We know that the Celts were a non-literate people who shared their history and legends through storytelling and song as far back as 1200 BCE, but there are traces of the Cailleach's symbolism in Spain, Greece, Portugal, and southern India that could date all the way back to the Neolithic period (7000 BCE). It's likely enough that the Cailleach got a similar treatment to the Baba Yaga: from a revered goddess to an ugly old witch with ambiguous intentions. Even today, though, the Cailleach's grumpiness seems to be a part of her charm, as it is one of the few consistent features of her tales.

The Cailleach's name, her blue skin, her red teeth, and her clothing decorated with skulls all invoke the Hindu goddess Kali, a fierce destroyer goddess who is connected to Dhumavati. We also see the Baba Yaga here, especially when the Cailleach is in the role of forest protector. She'll leave you alone well enough if you're respectful, but if you mess with any of her forest creatures, you'd better watch out. In that same role, we are reminded of the Greek hunter goddess Artemis, who represented the wildness and danger of the forest.

There is also an echo of Persephone and Demeter in the dance of Brigid and the Cailleach, especially as a story that explains the turning of the seasons. The story is inspired by a Scottish legend that often places Brigid and the Cailleach as enemies. In these versions, the Cailleach imprisons Brigid in the cave and makes her do impossible tasks she is only able to complete with supernatural help (recalling Vasilisa's corn and poppy seeds). Aengus plays the role of the rescuing prince, and Brigid and the Cailleach alternate their seasonal rule by battle or trickery, with Brigid prevailing on Beltane (May 1st) and the Cailleach taking over on Samhain (October 31st/ November 1st).

As the Queen of Winter, the Cailleach is always paired with Brigid, the Goddess of Spring, birth, creativity, and potential. She is the Maiden to the Cailleach's Crone. In some stories, the Cailleach *is* Brigid after she takes a drink from the magical Well of Youth on the Green Isle in the Otherworld, and slowly ages throughout the turning of the Wheel of the Year. In this case, like Inanna and Ereshkigal, Persephone and Demeter, Dhumavati and Sati, the two goddesses are merely different aspects of the same energy.

In a way, this story is a sort of inversion of Persephone and Demeter's. Where Persephone felt a call to the dark Underworld away from the bright abundance of her mother's world, Brigid felt a call to melt her mother's winter world and create Summerland. In both cases, the stability of the cycle relies on the turning of dark to light and back again, from birth to death and back to rebirth. The Maiden needs the Crone and the Crone needs the Maiden. Death gives life as life gives death, over and over again throughout the long eternity of the world.

THE CAILLEACH: THE ULTIMATE CRONE

The Cailleach may indeed be the oldest of the oldest Crones. She is the ultimate wise woman who knows all, has seen all, even gave birth to all. She was there at the beginning and she will be there at the end. Like the Baba Yaga, she can be a teacher to those who are willing to really listen (and will make short work of those who don't). Part of that listening means being able to see past the illusion of ugliness and giving this old hag a kiss. She is the Queen of Winter, the Goddess of the Snow. She holds the most elemental powers of darkness, earth, and cold, creating the landscape and everything in it at her whim.

Like many of our nature goddesses, the Cailleach is neither good nor bad, she is merely powerful. Nature is like that: it can be the softness of a summer day or the whipping winds of a winter night. She warns us of the mistake of wanting to stay in summer all year long: of insisting on seeing only the bright side, of soaking in hope and suppressing our sadness, of going and going without stopping to rest. She may come to our aid (or smack some sense into us) if we forget to honor our darker sides. Our pain, our fear, our difficult past—this is the rich soil that nurtures our resilience, hope, and sense of capability. Of course we want to enjoy what's light and sweet. But we can't do that if we don't understand the bitter.

MEDITATION WITH THE CAILLEACH:

Inviting the wisdom of the crone

Set your circle and make your land acknowledgment. Consider the land you are on, the lands of the Cailleach, and your relationship with these parts of the world. Light a candle if you like and have a journal and a pen nearby.

Invite into your circle a very old version of you, a version of you in your Crone era—an older, wiser version of you (any gender) who has been through it all. Take your time to notice whatever it is you discover about this older you.

Then invite in a Maiden version of you, a younger, more innocent self with all the potential in the world, but lacking, perhaps, some wisdom (again, don't worry too much about gender).

Allow these two to talk to each other and witness their conversation. If you like, you could write a letter from Maiden to Crone and then Crone to Maiden, and then read back what you've written.

When this feels complete, thank these versions of you and let them go. Sit with any learnings, noticings, or wisdom that came through the conversation. Close the circle and bow to the Cailleach, along with the Maiden, Warrior, Mother, and Crone in your own heart.

THE GODDESS CYCLE

This book opened with Persephone, a Maiden who transforms into the Queen of the Underworld. It closes with the Cailleach, the oldest Crone, whose wisdom grows only when she learns from the Maiden. The Crone eats the Maiden, perhaps, on the dark moon, but only so she can give birth to her again the next day as Mother. This is not the end of the goddess cycle, it is simply a moment in the endless circle, a phase in the perpetually cycling moon, a tale that will keep being told as long as there are people to listen. Go back and read Persephone, if you like, or start all over again with Skywoman or Lilith. There is no real beginning as there is no real end. This book, like the Goddess, is not a line with a period at the end. It is a circle.

The Goddess has always been what the people needed her to be. From the beginnings of human civilization, she held the mysteries of birth and death. She embodied the cycling of the seasons, the day, and the Moon. She is our potential as Maiden, our power as Warrior, our abundance as Mother, and our wisdom as Crone. She even shows us how to shapeshift when we are rejected, suppressed, and oppressed, even if that means going by a different name. She doesn't care what we call her or what face we give her (and she has countless more). She will be exactly who we need her to be when we need her. Whether we are in Egypt, Turtle Island, or the shallow Red Sea, the Goddess is telling our stories.

Our stories—and our identities—are as multiple as she is. As we watch the Goddess transform from the paleolithic Venus to Inanna and Ishtar and then the Virgin Mary, we are also watching ourselves, our ancestors, both colonizers and colonized, move into different lands, inserting themselves into the old stories, and fighting against erasure through mythically rebellious rememberings. A myth is supposed to be fluid, cyclic, to be able to evolve with the people, to mean something to the people who live now, not then. When it is written down and deemed authoritative, it can't move, it can't grow like a seed, it gets stuck, frozen in time and place, not allowing the medicinal evolutions it needs to serve the changing people.

So allow these stories to be seeds, not icicles. Let them grow and shift and change inside your heart. Feel into them now, and let them feel different later. Talk about them, tell them to your friends, your children, tell and retell them for yourself. You are a part of this cycle, this revolution. These stories are yours.

ENDNOTES

1 These are the opening lines to the Sumerian poem "The Descent of Inanna," dated around 1800 BCE, as quoted from *Inanna: Queen of Heaven and Earth: Her Stories and Hymns from Sumer* by Diane Wolkstein and Samuel Noah Kramer.

2 This exchange is paraphrased from the original poem as written in Wolkstein and Kramer.

3 Anna's lamentation is quoted directly from The Gospel of James.

BIBLIOGRAPHY

Brant, Beth, "This is History", *Gendered Intersections: An Introduction to Women's and Gender Studies* (Fernwood Publishing, Halifax NS, 2011)

Bruchac, Joseph, *Native American Stories* (Fulcrum Publishing, Golden CO, 1991)

Cashford, Jules and Baring, Anne, *The Myth of the Goddess: Evolution of an Image* (Penguin Books, London UK, 1991)

Chinnaiyan, MD, Kavitha M., *Shakti Rising: Embracing Shadow and Light on the Goddess Path to Wholeness* (New Harbinger Publications, Oakland CA, 2017)

Conway, D.J., *Maiden, Mother, Crone: The Myth and Reality of the Triple Goddess* (Llewellyn Publications, Woodbury MN, 1993)

Estes, Clarissa Pinkola, *Women Who Run with the Wolves: Myths and Stories of the Wild Woman Archetype* (Ballantine Books, New York NY, 1992)

Federici, Silvia, *Caliban and the Witch: Women, the Body, and Primitive Accumulation* (Autonomedia, Brooklyn NY, 2004)

Freeman, Philip, *Celtic Mythology: Tales of Gods, Goddesses, and Heroes* (Oxford University Press, Oxford UK, 2017)

Harris, Stephen L. and Platzner, Gloria, *Classic Mythology: Images and Insights, 3rd edition* (McGraw-Hill, Boston MA, 2004)

Hirschmann, Kris, *Monsters and Mythical Creatures: Medusa* (ReferencePoint Press, San Diego CA, 2011)

Hurwitz, Siegmund, *Lilith—The First Eve: Historical and Psychological Aspects of the Dark Feminine* (Daimon Verlag, Einsiedeln, Switzerland, 1992)

Johns, Andreas, *Baba Yaga: The Ambiguous Mother and Witch of the Russian Folktale* (Peter Lang Publishing, New York NY, 2004)

Kempton, Sally, *Awakening Shakti: The Transformative Power of the Goddesses of Yoga* (Sounds True, Boulder CO, 2013)

Kimmerer, Robin Wall, *Braiding Sweetgrass: Indigenous Wisdom, Scientific Knowledge, and the Teachings of Plants* (Milkweed Editions, Minneapolis MN, 2013)

Lockerbie, Savannah, "The Cailleach" episode of *The White Witch Podcast*

Madame Pamita, *Baba Yaga's Book of Witchcraft: Slavic Magic from the Witch of the Woods* (Llewellyn Publications, Woodbury MN, 2022)

Meyers, Carol, *Rediscovering Eve: Ancient Israelite Women in Context* (Oxford University Press, Oxford UK, 2013)

Monaghan, Patricia, *The Encyclopedia of Celtic Mythology and Folklore* (Facts on File, New York NY, 2004)

Patterson, Rachel, *Pagan Portals: The Cailleach* (Moon Books, Winchester UK, 2016)

Shenandoah, Joanne, and George-Kanentiio, Douglas M., *Skywoman: Legends of the Iroquois* (Clear Light Publishing, Santa Fe NM, 1998)

Spretnak, Charlene, *Lost Goddesses of Early Greece: A Collection of Pre-Hellenic Myths* (Beacon Press, Boston MA, 1978)

Stone, Merlin, *When God Was a Woman* (Harcourt Brace Jovanovich, New York NY, 1976)

Tower Hollis, Susan, "Women of Ancient Egypt and the Sky Goddess Nut", *The Journal of American Folklore* (University of Illinois Press, on behalf of the American Folklore Society, Urbana IL, 1990)

Warner, Marina, *Alone of All Her Sex: The Myth and Cult of the Virgin Mary* (Oxford University Press, Oxford UK, 1976)

Weber, Courtney, *The Morrígan: Celtic Goddess of Magic and Might* (Weiser Books, Newburyport MA, 2019)

Wells, R. A., "The Mythology of Nut and the Birth of Ra", *Studien zur Altägyptischen Kultur* (Helmut Buske Verlag, Hamburg, Germany, 1992)

Wolkstein, Diane and Kramer, Samuel Noah, *Inanna, Queen of Heaven and Earth: Her Stories and Hymns From Sumer* (Harper & Row, New York NY, 1983)

ACKNOWLEDGMENTS

Deep thanks to Lizzie Kaye for being willing to entertain all my ideas and turn them into something beautiful I can hold in my hands. My agent Robert Lecker is a friend, a mentor, and an advocate, and I am so grateful for his help and encouragement. Thank you to Olivia Davies, Jacqui Willcocks, and Megan Laven for sharing their thoughts, ideas, resources, and reactions. Aimee Bailey, Spokesperson of the Circle of Turtle Lodge, and Karen Goodfellow, award-winning contemporary First Nations artist and counseling therapist, consulted on the Skywoman chapter. Natalie Rousseau, one of my witchy mentors, generously shared her version of Persephone's story with me so I could write with it in mind. Thank you to Jane Trollope for her wonderful editing help and Nadia Murash for bringing the images of the Goddess to life in such magical detail, and to Victoria Allen and the whole team at David and Charles/Verbena. Any errors in this book are mine and mine alone.

Last but not least, thank you to my family, my parents Jane and Mike, my husband Rob, and my delightful son Grant, for all their support and care. Deep bows to the ancestors and all the stories they tell.

ABOUT THE AUTHOR

Julie Peters is a counseling therapist, tarot reader, and yoga and meditation teacher living and working on Plains Cree land in Treaty 6 territory, also known as Edmonton, Alberta, Canada. She is a staff writer for *Spirituality and Health Magazine* and has dozens of guided meditations on the Insight Timer meditation app. Julie is the author of *Secrets of the Eternal Moon Phase Goddesses: Meditations on Desire, Relationships, and the Art of Being Broken*, the Canada Book Award-winning *Want: 8 Steps to Recovering Desire, Passion, and Pleasure After Sexual Assault*, and *The Full Moon Yearbook: A Year of Ritual and Healing Under the Full Moon*. Learn more at www.juliepeters.ca.

INDEX

A VERBENA BOOK

Verbena is an imprint of David and Charles, Ltd
Suite A, Tourism House, Pynes Hill, Exeter, EX2 5WS

First published in the UK and USA in 2025

A catalogue record for this book is available from the British Library.

ISBN-13: 9781446314593 paperback
ISBN-13: 9781446314609 EPUB

This book has been printed on paper from approved suppliers and made from pulp from sustainable sources.

Printed in China by Leo Paper Products Ltd for:
David and Charles, Ltd
Suite A, Tourism House, Pynes Hill, Exeter, EX2 5WS

10 9 8 7 6 5 4 3 2 1

Publishing Director: Ame Verso
Senior Commissioning Editor: Lizzie Kaye
Publishing Manager: Jeni Chown
Editor: Victoria Allen
Copy Editor: Jane Trollope
Design: Sam Staddon
Pre-press Designer: Susan Reansbury
Illustrations: Nadia Murash
Production Manager: Beverley Richardson

David and Charles publishes high-quality books on a wide range of subjects. For more information visit www.davidandcharles.com.

Follow us on Instagram by searching for @dandcbooks.

Layout of the digital edition of this book may vary depending on reader hardware and display settings.